Unconventional Uncommon Unfamiliar

The Breakthrough Files

Chetan Walia

All rights reserved. No part of this Publication may be reproduced, stored in a retrieval system, or transmitted in any form or by any means, electronic, mechanical, photocopying or otherwise, without the prior permission of the copyright owner.

ISBN-13: 978-1717486660

ISBN-10: 1717486665

© ChetanWalia 2015
www.ChetanWalia.com
www.PitchPlan.com

Dedicated to Ma, who very early on taught me the most precious lesson, "be rough and tough" – this would go on to be my foundation. Rise or fall, get up, dust yourself out, believe and begin again. There couldn't be a more simplistic way to get to a breakthrough.

Contents

Preface

Section-1: Leadership
1. 44 Questions For Business Leaders
2. Leadership Impetus
3. Leadership Excellence – The Versus List
4. Decidedly Important Stuff
5. Leadership Lessons From Cricket

Section-2: Breakthroughs
6. A Breakthrough For You
7. Nothing Beats Action
8. The Get Lucky List
9. Be Your Own Santa
10. Ignore Your Mother. Ignore Your Father
11. The Winners Dozen
12. How Do You Succeed

Section-3: Management
13. This Is (or should be) Management
14. The Great Management Bullshit
15. CEOs Are Idiots When
16. Culture Of Sustainable Entrepreneurship

Section-4: Innovation & Change
17. Innovate Or Perish
18. Is Your organization open to Change
19. Damn HR
20. I Am Responsible
21. Life Is Not A Spectator Sport

Section-5: Sales & Marketing
22. The Great Salespeople
23. 50 Key lessons In Sales And In Marketing
24. Presentation Excellence

Top Quotes

Preface

This is not a book that flows from one chapter to another.

This is

Unconventional

Uncommon

Unfamiliar

These are my breakthrough files. These are lists. These are thoughts. This is uncommon sense because simple seems to be uncommon today.

Most of these are thoughts that have emanated from reading something or being exposed to some thought or the other. These are insights from my experience and learning.

The book is written as bullet point lists. While the reader may be able to read this quickly, it will take time to reflect and ponder over each point carefully. Each point here and collectively, represents a potential transformation.

These files break away from the norm and challenge you to challenge the mindless conformism and move over to do the right thing, the simple one.

I haven't edited my writing (or hired an editor to make everything polite) as conventionally would be the norm and as I have done for my previous writings. I deliberately wanted to keep this unfamiliar and lay the focus on the content. The reading experience might itself be unconventional.

What follows essentially is pure common sense. You will see that it is. What you will also realize as you read through this is how uncommon it is to do the simple things.

The book is categorized into insights in leadership, breakthroughs, management, innovation & change and sales & marketing.

I wish you the very best and hope to see you as unconventional, uncommon and unfamiliar.

1

44 Questions For Business Leaders
Section 1: Leadership

A reporter asked me to think about "a couple of questions a CEO ought to ask her/himself." I stopped—for now—at 46

1. **Can you imagine your tombstone having your company's performance results carved in it?** Of course you can't. (I hope) So what would you like on the tombstone? Why do you keep discussing numbers instead?

2. **How would you explain 'why you do' - what you do to your 10-year-old daughter?** (Aim for 25/50 words or less).

3. **How would you explain your most recent major decision to your 10-year-old daughter?** (Aim for 25/50 words or less).

4. **Did you miss half your 13-year-olds soccer games or school plays this year?** (I'll guarantee that if you live to be 100, you'll never forgive yourself no matter how many zeros in your net worth.)

5. **What does this really say about your priority setting, time management and leadership?**

6. **Are your training courses so damn good that they make you feel 'future ready'?**

7. **Can every employee, when stopped by you in the hall, describe her or his personal development strategy for 2014?** (Is it radical?).

8. **Is your CTO/Chief Training Officer on a par (pay, perks, pecking order) with your CFO/CIO/CMO?**

9. Have you (I HOPE) read *Forbes* publisher Rich Karlgaard's superb - **The Soft Edge?**

10. Do you have enough freaky customers in your portfolio, pushing you to the limit day in and day out?

11. If you got run over by a bus, could you guarantee that your successor is BETTER than you are?

12. Have you thanked 10 people for SOMETHING ... today?

13. At year's end do you call 25-50 people to thank them for their support during the prior 12 months? (Inspired by Hank Paulson)

14. **Is EVERY meeting a Paragon of Excellence?** To a large extent, like it or not, meetings are ALL that you do. Sadly but Truly.

15. **Do you ever act like an asshole?** Guess what, dude, you can't get away with it—you are NOT Steve Jobs.

16. **Do you have an implicit bias for capital investments over people investments?** Think VERY carefully about this.

17. **Are you a good listener?** Odds are VERY high that you are not—AND that you're getting worse. Nothing is more important. It is a subject that can be studied and mastered.

18. Are you a PROFESSIONAL - listener?

19. Are you a PROFESSIONAL - at hiring?

20. Are you a PROFESSIONAL - at evaluating people?

21. How many-off-the-charts crazy new people have you had lunch with in the last 90 days?

22. **Do you read enough?** (THE answer is "No.")

23. **If all of your traditional marketing programs were shut down tomorrow, would your extant Social Media programs carry the load?**

24. **Do you think the whole "social media"/"social employee"/"social business" "thing" is overblown?** It may be, but are you sure? Good chance it's "under blown." How do you plan to test the overblown/under blown hypothesis?

25. **Do you insist on too much data too have a discussion or to make decisions?** Sure enough you want facts. But are you so lazy and grounded in your chair that apart from that data, you have very little conviction about what's going on?

26. **Do you make eye contact 100% of the time?**

27. **Do you meet your customers every week?**

28. **To what degree can you say you are honestly** (regularly, intensively) **in touch with folks three levels "down" in the organization—where the real work gets done?**

29. **Are you over-reliant on email, or do you still use the phone regularly?**

30. **Do you reward imaginative failures that lead to significant learning?** Courtesy a successful Aussie exec who says his philosophy is, "Reward excellent failures, punish mediocre successes."

31. **Do you have a rigid/near-religious routine of calling a key contact at each of your top 10 (25) customers once a**

month?

32. **Are you sure that you are not so intimidating that you cause people not to share priority problems with you early on when they are fixable?** Hint, you think you are approachable—odds are you are alone in that assessment.

33. Women buy the lion's share of retail AND commercial goods. **Does your top team reflect that?** (If it doesn't, you're outdated).

34. **Is your top team a paragon of diversity?** Or do they all have SIMILAR backgrounds with SIMILAR education, coming up with SIMILAR ideas and SIMILAR problems?

35. **Have you read and attentively studied and widely shared Daniel Kahneman's book Thinking, Fast and Slow?** It will shake your confidence in your and your colleagues' judgment/decision-making skills—that's a good thing.

36. **Do you think your intuition is good?** I don't think so —and I don't even know you.

37. **Is 50% of your time unscheduled?** (Courtesy Intel superstar Dov Frohman's book *Leadership the Hard Way*. Frohman says over-scheduling and failure to "daydream" are CEOs' two top failings.)

38. **Is your full cadre of 1st-line bosses staggeringly talented and well trained/mentored/compensated?** The population of 1st-line bosses is unmistakably the #1 determinant of productivity/employee retention.

39. **Do you have an implicit bias toward noisy, aggressive people?** You probably do. Read the book *Quiet*—and realize

that shortchanging introverts is a strategic mistake.

40. **Do you acknowledge that failed cross-functional communication/cooperation/ synergy is the #1 cause of delays of … EVERYTHING?** (It is) Do you work VISIBLY on this EVERY day?

41. **Do you acknowledge that there are about 500 ways to de-motivate people, and about 5 ways to motivate them—and act accordingly?**

42. **Do you quickly get tired of people who constantly say, "the sky is falling"?** Well, I do, too. But sometimes it is falling. I pray you are an optimist; I pray that you have a few pessimistic pals whom you do not dismiss out of hand.

43. **Do you acknowledge that acquisitions rarely live up to their billing—the billing that was so gloriously touted by you?** And do you acknowledge that when acquisitions blow up it is usually courtesy a "culture clash" which you didn't look at hard enough during the vetting process? (If you don't acknowledge that, you are wrong. PERIOD.)

44. **In presentations you review, is there as much/more text devoted to implementation as there is to problem/opportunity analysis?**

45. **In presentations that you review, are you more worried about 'what went wrong' versus 'what are you going to do about it'?** Where does you time go?

46. **Is your strategic plan > 2 pages?**
    If yes - shame on you.

2

Leadership Impetus

Section 1: Leadership

The Impetus To Lead – Leadership 25

The Basic Premise

1. **Leadership Is a - Mutual Discovery Process.**

    "Ninety percent of what we call 'management' consists of making it difficult for people to get things done." – Peter Drucker

The Leadership Types

2. Great Leaders on Snorting Steeds Are Important – but **Great Talent Developers** (Type I Leadership) **are the Bedrock of Organizations** that Perform Over the Long Haul.

3. But Then Again, There Are Times When This **"Cult of Personality"** (Type II Leadership) **Stuff Actually Works!**

    "A leader is a dealer in hope." – Napoleon

4. **Find the "Businesspeople"!** *(Type III Leadership)*

IPM – Inspired Profit Mechanic

5. All organizations need the **Golden Leadership Triangle.**

    The Golden Leadership Triangle: (1) Talent Fanatic - (2) Creator-Visionary - (3) Inspired Profit Mechanic.

The Leadership Dance

6. Leaders **DO.**
7. Leaders **RE-do.**

"If Microsoft is good at anything, it's avoiding the trap of worrying about criticism. Microsoft fails constantly. They're eviscerated in public for lousy products. Yet they persist, through version after version, until they get something good enough. Then they leverage the power they've gained in other markets to enforce their standard." - Seth Godin, Zooming

8. Leaders **Love The Mess.**

"I'm not comfortable unless I'm uncomfortable." - Jay Chiat

9. Leaders **are Optimists.**

10. Leaders **Focus.**

" I used to have a rule for myself that at any point in time I wanted to have in mind — as it so happens, also in writing, on a little card I carried around with me — the three big things I was trying to get done. Three. Not two. Not four. Not five. Not ten. Three." — Richard Haass, The Power to Persuade

To Don't Lists
If It Isn't Broke, Break It.

11. Leaders send **V-E-R-Y Clear Signals.**

12. Leaders **Forget.** Leaders **Destroy.**

Forget > Learn

"The problem is never how to get new, innovative thoughts into your mind, but how to get the old ones out." - Dee Hock

13. Leaders **Forget.** Leaders **Destroy.**

14. **But Leaders Have to Deliver,** so they worry about "throwing the bay out with the bath water."

Fail. Fast.

15. Leaders **make mistakes** (LOTS) and **make no bones** about it.

16. Leaders **Make their Mark.** Leaders **Do Stuff That Matters.**

Create A Cause. Not A Business.

"I never, ever thought of myself as a businessman. I was interested in creating things I would be proud of." - Richard Branson

17. Leaders have a **Great Story.**

" A key – perhaps the key – to leadership is the effective communication of a story." - Howard Gardner, Leading Minds: An Anatomy of Leadership

Talent

18. When it comes to **Talent – Leaders Never Compromise.**

19. Leaders don't create **'Followers'** – they create **'Leaders'**

20. Leaders **GIVE Respect.**

Passion

21. Leaders **Openly Display Their Passion.**

"Nothing is so contagious as enthusiasm." —Samuel Taylor Coleridge

22. Leaders **are in a Hurry.**

"If things seem under control, you're just not going fast enough."—Mario Andretti

23. Leaders know its **All Sales All The Time.**

If you don't LOVE SALES ... find another life. (Don't pretend you're a "leader.")

24. Leadership is an **Authentic Performance.**

"You must be the change you wish to see in the world." - Gandhi

25. Leaders **Open the Possibilities**

"Beware of the tyranny of making Small Changes to Small Things. Rather, make Big Changes to Big Things." —Roger Enrico, former Chairman, PepsiCo

"You can't behave in a calm, rational manner. You've got to be out there on the lunatic fringe." — Jack Welch

3

Leadership Excellence
The 'Versus' List

Convention versus Uncommon Sense
Section 1: Leadership

1. Politics as nuisance-distraction **versus "Politics Is Life. RELISH It."**

2. **IQ > EQ versus EQ > IQ.** Can You Really Choose? Reality you need high IQ. And you need EQ=IQ

3. Buttoned down to a fault **versus "I am a dispenser of Enthusiasm."**

4. "We don't have time for niceties" **versus Civility. Always.** An Uncivil Person as a CEO seems to be fashionable. It destroys, destructs and destabilizes performance.

5. What Shall We Do Next **versus Embrace Madness**

6. People resist change (Cliché) **versus No one resists it.** They just don't understand it. This is your fault.

7. One step at a time **versus Giant Leaps.** What's the logic? When you can take four, why wouldn't you?

8. Choose. Optimistic or Bust **versus Under Promise or Bust.**

9. In office **versus Out of office or No office.** Really, what part of your business is conducted within?

10. Your meetings are pain in the butt **versus Meetings is a leadership opportunity #1.**

11. Formal customer-vendor relationships **versus "No Barriers" – fully integrated partnerships.**

12. No distractions please – I have a secretary for all this. **Boy, you**

are such a whiny pig.

13. Information as needed **versus Wildly over communicate with everyone.**

14. Confidentiality is necessary **versus** Confidentiality is 99% nonsense. **Inform everyone about everything.** Life is easier.

15. Email **versus Face-to-Face.** HINT - Would You Like If Your Children Informed You On Email - "Dad, I decided to quit college. Out of time. Will explain at the end of FY."

16. Overscheduled **versus 50% Unscheduled time.**

17. Best department **versus Cross Functional Excellence.** Your #1 Job.

18. Recognition as deserved **versus Recognition, especially for little stuff.** Celebrate every damn milestone imaginable. Make 'em up if need be.

19. Talk **versus Listen.** Listening is strategic tool #1.

20. "Here's the deal." **versus "What Do You Think?"** The four most powerful words in an organization – what do you think.

21. I have hired good people so there's little need for training **versus training is my Investment #1.**

22. Noisy **versus Quiet.** Introverts are under represented in your team. Fix it.

23. Leaders are first and foremost paid to deliver business results **versus Leaders are in the people development business.**

24. Bosses aim to help people be successful **versus Bosses make people grow.**

25. Our core team has more men than women **versus Women are best leaders. Period.**

26. Concentration. No nonsense **versus Daydreaming. Reading. Freaky Fridays.**

27. Kaizen **vs. WOWification.**

28. Make a damn good product **versus Good product is a threshold requirement. Integrated services.**

29. Good work **vs. Excellence.**

30. Performance management system **versus Entrepreneurial mindset.**

4

Decidedly Important Stuff
Section 1: Leadership

Well, it may not all be brilliant, but I do believe there is some "stuff" within that could improve your organization/business/ leadership practice as this year performs its madcap opening act.

(The context of the changing economy and changing technology means that no individual or organization can sit on a pat hand. So, I repeat, do use the beginning of this year to assess where you are.)

1. **Change.** A lot is said on change. 99.99999% of what is said is negative. Do yourself a favor - Surround yourself with people who will welcome changes you want to make in life. Don't allow you to be distracted or sidetracked by foes. MOVE.

2. **Do good work.** You'll spend most of your hours at work. Make the best of it—or you will have thrown away your life. (Strong words. Warranted) - Don't like your work THEN Don't spend your life there.

3. **Begin your day on a high.** Bring a SMILE to work. First TEN MINUTES determine the flow of the day.

4. **Close the day with a bang.** As long as you feel successful at the end of the day your day was worthwhile, else it was scrap value. Do things that make you feel successful - **(even if apart from work).**

5. **Learning.** One of the finest ways to feel successful is to learn something new. Read. Train. Interact. Learn.

6. **Help People.** Don't let anything get in the way of helping others to grow. Help them achieve more than they thought they could. (HINT: You'll make a lot of money along the way)

7. **The "secret."** That's the secret to happiness in families too - Help Grow. Far too often we are busy establishing supremacy in families. If only we helped, we'd be happy people.

8. **Be happy.** Celebrate. Smile. Joy. Laugh. Live. Damn it. (Why not?) When will you?

9. **WOW. The rule that never will fail.** The more WOWS you can create, the more WOW will life be to you. Personal and Professional. Try it.

10. **First–line Leadership.** The #1 determining productivity is the quality of 1st-line leaders. (Recruit 'em and train 'em accordingly).

11. **The 'S' Factor. SOCIAL FACTOR.** You like it or not, business will be transacted on 'social' media in the future. In the present. Whether its organization business or whether its landing a job for you. Get on the train.

12. **Giving.** The more you give unconditionally, the more you get unconditionally. Applies to anything - love or money. You wouldn't know, right?

13. **This defines YOU.** We are indeed what we eat—and who we spend time with.

14. **This defines YOU FURTHER.** Your Calendar. You ARE how you spend your time. PERIOD.

15. **Be Civil.** I didn't think I'll ever have to write this. But it is **TOTALLY** missing in these times. From the TV studio to the Metro ride, civility is dead and buried. I have an opportunity to present to you - Civility can be a **STUNNING** competitive

advantage.

16. **Politics. GET OVER IT.** Doesn't help you. Doesn't make for a happy day. Life wasted.

17. **"Excellent" Meetings.** Meetings are what bosses "do." Excellent Meetings are what leaders do. Act accordingly.

18. **Email Excellence.** Your biggest 'in front of people' tool today is email. Why wouldn't you be excellent at it? Really, why not?

19. **Reaction > Action.** How you react is more important. The act has already happened.

20. **Thank you!** A leader uses the two words magically. An arrogant fool rarely does. At the end of the day, all that will matter is genuine respect. Earn.

21. **Thank You Power.** Power is awesome, right? Thank you (acknowledgement) is the simplest way to get it. Think.

22. **Listen!** Make 2014: The **Year of the EAR.**

23. **WRITE.** You don't have to publish. Writing is the biggest tool for self-awareness.

24. **52 Weeks - Every Week.** BEGINNINGS and ENDINGS matter. A LOT.

25. **We are really good at faultfinding.** It sucks. The one who progresses finds solutions.

26. **Leaders exist to serve.** Period. I don't see one in Politics. Yuck.

27. **Strategy is boardroom time pass. Winners spend that time on execution.**

28. **Radical Personal Development.** It's the only survival strategy amidst the economic/tech tsunami. Start ASAP.

29. **Be ready.** Being ready means to not resist when opportunities come. Our first response to anything is usually a skeptical one.

30. **Judgment.** Our judgment stinks. Period. Want Proof - Take a look at our politicians.

31. **Culture comes first.** Former IBM CEO Lou Gerstner says it, it must be so ~ your culture determines your profits, not your strategy.

32. **The Rule.** If your organization or your career is not built on integrity - It will self-destruct. (Study any part or all of history).

33. **The Personal Impact.** Integrity and Ethics isn't situational. Can you teach your kids that be situational about integrity? FACT: they will learn anyways by seeing you. Unless you change.

34. **Biggest Life Decision.** Your call. Be non negotiable on integrity or be forgotten even while you're alive. Your call.

35. **Read! Read! Read some more!** One of the premier investment bankers in the world declares CEOs' #1 problem to be a failure to read enough.

36. **The last word.** People First—or else nothing.

37. **The last word (Part-2).** Do (NOW) or Die without it ever being done.

38. **The last word (Part-3).** The only thing we have to fear is the absence of fear.

39. **The LAST word (Part-4).** You are as brilliant as your 'integrity'. If you don't have it, eventually everyone will TRASH you.

40. **Nobody knows anything.** Hmmmmm.

5

Leadership Lessons From Cricket
Section 1: Leadership

Fans cheer and sing for their favorite team. Known as a national obsession and even labeled as alternate religion in India, cricket season starts with incredible hope for all teams equally and goes from spring to summer to winter, until the top team emerges.

I am a loyal, diehard, devoted Indian cricket fan and have been since my father bought me my first cricket bat at three years of age.

What does all this have to do with your business and leadership? Lots. I once saw Sachin Tendulkar batting and started writing this. It has **PLENTY** to do with business and leadership. Study the games, the teams, the players, the cricket and you will discover amazing similarities to your career.

Here are the lessons in Cricket you can apply to your business game once you understand the importance and impact:

1. **Cricket teams are made of individual players who learn how to play together.** The individual skills contribute to the team's success. They cannot win alone. The best team wins. **Doesn't this make the primary job of a leader to build people rather than deliver numbers?**

2. **Every great player was once a beginner.** They started at a young age because they loved to play. **It's always learnt through experience – cricket or leadership.**

3. **Every international cricketer started in some 'unheard of' club in your neighborhood. In cricket, like in business, there aren't any shortcuts; you have to work your way up.**

4. **Cricketers are coachable.** Being coached, listening and learning from coaches, seniors and other players in other teams are keys to success. **Listening is strategy and skill #1.**

5. **Players warm up and practice before EVERY game.** Even if they have been playing for years, they practice before every game. **Where do you refresh your skills?**

6. **Cricketers learn the fundamentals, the basics of the game until they are automatic.** Then they practice them every day. Fundamentals like: keep your eye on the ball. Catching practice. Net practice. Foot forward. Know the rules. Know the plan. Implement the plan. How many times in a post match interview have you heard the winning captain say – "We did the basics right." **What are your basics for business? Are you even aware of them, leave alone automation?**

7. **All cricketers, even the greatest of them, get into a slump.** Coaching, watching their own tapes, practice, determination and attitude gets them out of it. **Do you get better or do you quit?**

8. **All cricketers make errors.** Sometimes an error can cost you the game. Take errors seriously, NOT personally. Learn from them and don't repeat them. **Mistakes make you better – do you reprimand mistakes?**

9. **They love the game.** They love what they do and play to win. **Do your people love your game?**

Harsh Realities of Business and cricket

- Very few players who do make it to the international level, become leaders.

- Very few players get to be match winners.

- Small errors in judgment, three bad matches can cost you your career. In India even one's enough if you aren't Sachin Tendulkar.

- All cheaters eventually get caught.

- There is no champagne for second place.

- Fans become disenchanted when teams lose. Sad. But there's still a lesson: To keep them excited, you must keep yourself excited.

There are unspoken rules of the game – both in cricket and business. You got to believe in your team and teammates. You got to believe your team would win. You got to believe in your coach, your leader.

There are only 55 players (out of millions who play the game) in the Hall of Fame. **It takes years of dedication to earn that respect.**

6

A Breakthrough For You

Section 2: Breakthroughs

A few months back, three people I met have stayed in my memory and prompted me to simplify 'breakthroughs'.

First a highly successful man who is probably worth more than the net-worth of my entire client base combined - But this person considers himself unlucky and unsuccessful.

Second a person I have been coaching for the last one year who for the last 30 years dreamt of writing a book but never really started. Kept thinking. Last month in 7 days flat he authored his first book. Its being published by Penguin.

Third a gentleman seated next to me in the airplane who was training to climb the Everest. He says he has been training the last 3 years. Looks about 50 max. Super fit. Enviously built. I couldn't believe it when he told me his age. I still can't. He is 74 years old.

What a Breakthrough is not?

1. **Is not a sudden windfall or a sudden success.** (Even though my friend wrote a book in 7 days, it took years of preparation in the mind)

2. **Is not lottery luck.** Luck, yes! chance, no way!. Hard work. Sweat. Toil. Persistence.

3. **Is never, NEVER an isolated case.** Its almost impossible to experience a breakthrough in just a single area of your life. It transcends and multiplies itself.

4. **Has absolutely nothing to do with your successes and failures of the past.** As I wrote in the beginning - the richest and most successful man I know feels like he is a beggar and the oldest one who till the age of 60 never ever saw a gym is the

fittest person I have met in my life.

Two Rules to Accept If You Want to See A Breakthrough

1- All Reality is either false reasoning (or pure intellectualization to prevent breakthrough action) or pure imagination. All of it.

Whatever reason (or as you may call it - Fact) that you have that prevents you from taking action on producing a breakthrough is pure BS. 100% crap. Breakthrough can be anything - it can be losing 20 pounds of weight in 2 months or it can be doubling your income this year or it can be in your relationships or in your business growth. Whatever reasons you have that don't let you take action towards achieving your breakthrough, or, if you do take action, the reasons that why results aren't appearing are all figments of imagination. Its the liar in you in full swing.

Unless you accept this - Reason is 'YOU' - 100% - You will never see a breakthrough. You don't even need to read further.

2- Having accepted that the reason is 'you', now its important to remember that in generating breakthroughs, Frequency > Intensity.

It is not about putting in all your energy and effort in one go. It is not about running 10 miles in one shot on your first day. It is not about coming up with a whacko high voltage marketing strategy for your business. It is not about taking one great holiday with your spouse in a long time. It is not about a 'single' highly passionate action. That WILL NOT result in a breakthrough.

Frequency is greater than Intensity. Breakthrough comes with sustained action (everyday). It can be much smaller steps, but the continuity outperforms intensity.

How to Generate Breakthroughs In Life?

I have a very simple process. Its 4 Steps. Its simple but that does not in any way imply its easy. In my experience of doing this with people, I can tell you that it takes GUTS. You might read the following steps and think, "How on earth does this take guts?" - I'll tell you how - It takes guts to become 100% responsible - anyone can blame another person or situation - takes very little effort and is often liberating, though a wonderful act of cowardice.
It takes GUTS to be responsible to you.

Here are the four steps:

1- A Bold Intent. What is your Breakthrough? Is it Bold enough to be called a Breakthrough? Does it scare you, yourself and others around you that you want to do something or achieve something as crazy? If the answer is no to any of these questions, you wont see a breakthrough. You wont see a breakdown either but no breakthrough for sure.

I had a person recently in my workshop who wanted to lose 10 pounds in the next 3 years. He'll never lose it. Its not bold and it defies a rule above - it doesn't propel you to action everyday. You want a breakthrough - you dare to state that you want it in 50 days flat - and now you know exactly what you need to do everyday. If you say its not possible - Read Rule #1.

Place Your Intent: What do you want to achieve? What is your breakthrough?

a. State it.
b. Quantify it.

c. Make it bold.
   d. Is it getting your heart beating faster?
   e. If not, make it bolder,
   f. Check again.

One of the examples I quoted in the beginning was a 74-year-old man preparing to climb Everest. Will he do it? I don't care whether he'll reach the top or not but I'll tell you what - he'll damn well give it a shot. And that in itself is a breakthrough.

2- Initiative. My friend wanted to write a book for 30 years but did it in 7 days. You know what, at any point in the last 30 years, it would have taken 7 days. Sad. The only thing changed now was that he took action and didn't give up. In my mind there are three things that prevent initiative:

   i. Plain Laziness.

   ii. A story in the head - *'after such and such'*, 'not ready right now', 'too much else going on'

   iii. Fear of discovering failure- for example its nicer to have a story in the head that one fine day you'll be a best selling author than to write a book and find out that its not good enough. Or - its nicer to dream that its a matter of time before you hit the gym and get a great fit body than to actually hit it and want to quit in 3 days.

Initiative or the first action doesn't happen because you don't want to shatter your fairy tale - Read Rule#2.

Begin. Nothing will happen till you do. As Richard Branson wrote in his book 'even falling flat on your face is a step forward'

To be successful remember - Frequency of action is more important than Intensity of effort. Whatever you start - make sure you can do it everyday. Or don't begin, it won't succeed.

3- There is a price to pay. Pay it. Don't be fooled by the simplicity of this. Breakthroughs come at price. Mostly a price to pay in the short-term. Pay it.

I'll give you three recent examples here on we think:

First. In a recent coaching conversation I discovered that a highly successful person is unable to generate his breakthroughs in health because he feels he cannot get away from office to focus on that. My Rule says its BS reason so I probed. I found that he equates his 'input of effort at work' to the 'output he'll generate for the company' and thus maximize his chances to be the CEO. What crap! He is 44, looks 84 and will probably have a major health hazard before he walks to the CEOs cabin itself. There is a short-term price to pay here, probably. But without paying it he is neither becoming the CEO, nor getting healthier.

Second. I was working with the President of a leading bank. I wanted to change his aggressive behavior to a more empowering approach towards his subordinates. His first reaction - "its banking Sir, and you don't know the high egos here, the work will collapse." - again Rule-1 - all imagination.

Eventually you know what was preventing the change - 'if I do change this, what will people think? What suddenly happened to me? And wouldn't I be accepting that I was wrong in my approach up to now?"

Dealing with the Guilt of having been a certain way! - Yes it prevents any change. And Yes people will think that and will say 'I told you that you were wrong' - Deal with it. If its your price to pay - Pay It.

Third. Is not an example but a general statement. It works in our subconscious. When you do succeed at something, you boot out certain people and things from your life. We resist paying that price: For example - hitting a business breakthrough might mean changing a team and letting go of some people. Starting your own business might mean offending a few people around you. Getting better health means changing lifestyles and mostly becoming unsocial in the sort-term.

Breakthrough comes at a price. Not deciding to pay it comes at an even bigger price - that price is a rapidly declining self worth.

4- Feel Successful. Celebrate. I wrote about this richest person I met who feels unsuccessful and considers himself a failure. Here is why? - He is a second-generation entrepreneur so anything he achieves, everyone's reaction around him is - So What?

All his life success has been about getting recognition and appreciation from others - which hasn't come because people say - So What's the Big Deal?

He doesn't feel successful.

You might not too - all of us have areas where we don't - health, wealth, relationships, career ...

So what's the problem?

When you don't feel successful (every single day, remember the rules), your self worth (or self esteem) goes down. When self-esteem goes down, what decisions are you likely to take?

You can take this as a third rule of Breakthroughs if you may - **You take your worst and most self-sabotaging decisions when your self worth is down.**

So our rich friend here has all the money - but not enough self worth. What does he do? What decisions did he take? He has surrounded himself with 'yes' men who dare not question him. That has led to a standstill in business. He made sure his children were brought up with fear - he can't have his family now say 'so what' to him - they despise him now and want none of his business. Being depressed by that he drinks often and so has gained a lot of weight. He looks himself in the mirror and doesn't like the way he looks. Self worth goes further down. One more round of bad decisions begin.

It is vital to feel successful everyday. We make the mistake of putting our definitions of success so high (I'll be successful when I live in my Villa or drive my Ferrari) that we don't enjoy our small successes. And if we don't do that then naturally Self Worth goes down and obviously with it goes the breakthrough.

Here is what needs to be done:

1. Figure out your intent.
2. Figure out your daily action.
3. Pay the short-term price.
4. Feel Successful. Celebrate.

If your daily action is to for example walk for 30 minutes everyday then at the end of the day feel successful about it. Celebrate it. Be proud that you stayed on course.

Its a no brainer - only when you feel successful, will you do it everyday right? And only when you do it everyday will you get the result, right? Now if you know it, why don't you do it?

It all comes down to self-worth. If after knowing it, you are not doing it, then you obviously don't believe you deserve it.

It takes GUTS to see this within you. And that is the saddest and the simplest way that I can find to summarize why people don't see breakthroughs.

7
Nothing Beats Action
Section 2: Breakthroughs

The one thing (only) I've learnt for sure in consulting with people and businesses – Nothing beats action.

I am expanding this here below in many ways. See what sticks for you.

Ready. Steady. Go. (This you learnt at age 5)
This is far better than and works a lot more than "let's call a meeting and work it out."

Move fast, break things. (Facebook)
Breaking the norm produces a far bigger result than improving on the norm.

Example: Light bulb wasn't invented by improving the candle.

"You miss 100% of the shots you never take." (Wayne Gretzky)
Can Your Business Fail Fast Enough To Succeed? (*Economist* Conference Title)

Action. Action. Action.

You might fail. But if you don't take the shot, You Will Fail.

So no matter. Try again. Fail again. Fail better.
Do you talk about creating entrepreneur spirit? This is it.

Demo or die. (MIT Media Lab)
"We have a 'strategic plan.' It's called 'doing things.'" (Herb Kelleher -Southwest Airlines)

An Observation - With taking a decision to do something - comes responsibility to do it right - So what do most people do - Delay the decision - This happens subconsciously to over 80% of Executive

Decision Makers (or lack of them)

"Can do!" (Motto/U.S. Navy Seabees)
Opposite of this statement isn't Can't Do. It is 'am lazy or am scared."

Blame no one. Expect Nothing. Do something. (NFL coach Bill Parcells/locker-room poster)
"Ever noticed that *What the hell* is always the right decision?" (Anon - screenwriter)

Excuses may give you a reason or a justification. It never gives you the results.

Doing DOES.

Whoever Tries The Most Stuff Wins. (Reality).
The opposite of success - Play The Waiting Game.

Ready.
Steady.
Go.

Is this what you do?
H. Ross Perot/EDS founder, former GM board member "The first person to see a snake kills it. At GM, the first thing you do is organize a committee on snakes. Then you bring in a consultant who knows a lot about snakes. Third thing you do is talk about it for a year."

A Final Story.
A man approached J.P. Morgan, held up an envelope, and said, "Sir, in my hand I hold a guaranteed formula for success, which I will

gladly sell you for $25,000." "Sir," J.P. Morgan replied, "I do not know what is in the envelope, however if you show me, and I like it, I give you my word as a gentleman that I will pay you what you ask."

The man agreed to the terms, and handed over the envelope. J.P. Morgan opened it, and extracted a single sheet of paper. He gave it one look, a mere glance, and then handed the piece of paper back to the gent. And paid him the agreed-upon $25,000.

The formula:

1. Every morning, write a list of the things that need to be done that day.

2. **Do Them.**

8
The Get Lucky List
Section 2: Breakthroughs

I was just reading an old book (Liberation Management, pages 612–614) on my shelf that had this chapter on luck. It just fired my imagination and I just wrote my adapted version of this down.

Luck does play a big part in success. If you at times find yourself throwing your hands up in the air in despair, try a few of these strategies to get lucky.

If you are the planning types and believe meticulous and orderly plans are the only way forward and luck is just a by product, then by all means keep at it.

Have a little fun. Get lucky. Try these strategies.

1. **Chop off the cribbing.** Get on with something.

2. **Shoot it.** Don't just keep aiming.

3. **Fire one in the dark.** You never know.

4. "If a thing is worth doing, **it is worth doing badly.**"—G.K. Chesterton

5. **Just Start.**

6. **Read. Read. Read.**

7. Where you will be same time next year hugely depends on **what you will read and whom you will meet.**

8. Read stuff not just bestsellers. **Got to think differently.**

9. **Travel.** Visit new places. Insights guaranteed.

10. Just don't drink yourself nuts when you travel. **Then insights guaranteed.**

11. **Reinvent old hobbies.** Photography. Gardening. Sports. Whatever. Do.

12. **Take up a sport.** Have some fun.

13. Work with **weird people.**

14. **Ask really dumb questions.** "How come a CD can only take about 20 songs?" Somebody asked that stupid question and came up with an iPod.

15. **Failure is good.** It indicates that you stretch. Pursue a few failures of the past. Give it one more try. Just one. Do it in the craziest way you can think of. Go nuts.

16. **Have a 'different day' tomorrow.** Do everything that you normally do differently. That will get you thinking.

17. **Listen to everyone today.** Get ideas through questions.

18. **Don't listen to anyone today.** Just do what your gut says at supersonic mad speed.

19. **Get fired.** Maybe the best that will happen to you.

20. **Don't hang out with people who think they are unlucky.** It rubs off.

21. **Hang out with crazy people.**

22. **No idea ever came from a plan.** It just came. Free up your

mind. Get intuitive. How?

23. **Delegate** everything on your plate.

24. **Delegate more.** Have time.

25. **Destroy protocol.** Challenge your boss on something. Be intelligent. Have an outcome in mind. Go.

26. **Take a risk.** Go take someone from another function for lunch. Enjoy.

27. **Open up.** Make everyone like you. Bare all details at work. For example, if you are a business owner, make everyone a businessperson with access to all financials.

28. **Take a two-month break from work.** Please use that leave. Don't count pennies. Use them.

29. Spend 15 days out of every 30 - **OUTSIDE.** Customer. Vendor. Distributor. Whoever. BE OUT. The opportunities are there. They are not sitting on your conference table.

30. **Don't balance.** Don't let others balance. Spread confusion. Ask confusing questions.

31. **Disorganize.** Disorganize everything. Bureaucracy and Politics will break down.

32. **Attack your corporate culture.**

33. Encourage people to attack it too.

34. Loosen up.

35. Wear jeans to office. **Change things.** Be comfortable.

36. And then (AGAIN) **Get out of office.** Nothing inspiring happened at your table for as long as you have sat there. MOVE.

37. **Work from home for a week.**

38. **Don't help anyone.** Let people who work for you fall flat on their face and learn.

39. **"Life is either a daring adventure or nothing"**—Helen Keller - Dare Today. Something from this list. DO.

40. **Get the execution right.** The strategy will take care of itself.

41. **Disrespect tradition for a day.** Discover your own beliefs. Grow up.

42. **Start rewarding excellent failures.** Yours' too. They are worth far more than security.

43. **Celebrate a full day.** For what? For being alive.

44. **Success is relationships.** Period. Go work on two of them today.

45. **Observe children playing in a field.** Go see what you really were a few years back. Learn. You always had fun then.

46. **Join a public speaking forum.** Practice. Become confident. It's a big boost to ego.

47. Latest Fortune 500 report proves that **Women are better leaders than Men.** How many are there in your team?

48. **"Do one thing every day that scares you."**—Eleanor Roosevelt

49. **Do something that will make you feel that you are living, not just existing.** Do it now.

50. **"We eat change for breakfast!"**—Harry Quadracci, founder, QuadGraphics - That should be your plan for daily luck!! Keep changing it.

That's my 50. Do these come close to being you? Or do the opposites of this 50 come close to being you. I thought it might so here's number **51. Chill out.** Life isn't serious. Have some fun. Let go.

9

Be Your Own Santa
Section 2: Breakthroughs

I was seven years old when in the middle of the night on Christmas Eve, my eyes briefly opened and I saw my mother putting a present under my pillow. The secret was revealed. Oh my God, I was heartbroken. I had secretly asked my dear Santa for so much more. I knew I was not going to get it. It was a sad, weepy child who went back to sleep, now knowing that there is no Santa.

At the Christmas party the next morning, I tried explaining to all my friends that there is no Santa. I was proud to be making the discovery for them. They did not believe me. Not one of them. They had their reasons. I heard statements like:

"I asked for a bicycle, I got it."

"I asked for a cricket bat, I got it."

"I asked for chocolates, I got them."

I was all confused. What was I to believe in? Was there a Santa or not? Did I really see my mother at night? Or was I dreaming? Was my mother Santa?

Troubled as I was with all these questions and absolutely determined to solve the mystery, I approached my grandfather and told him all that had happened. I was even more flustered when I did not get a clear answer.

This must have shown on my face. Then he spoke. He said, **"Santa exists. He always will, but he exists in you. You have to be your own Santa."**

As a seven-year-old, I never understood that statement, but I wrote it in a notebook, as I had been asked to do: "Be your own Santa."

From that day on, these words would instantly pop up in my head every Christmas. Be your own Santa. I never understood what this meant or how you were supposed to do it. However, every year on the 25th of December I recited these words.

Twenty years later, I was in a toy store buying a Christmas gift for my three-year-old niece. Suddenly, I heard the words "be your own Santa" in my mind.

After leaving the store, I bought myself a Christmas present for the first time. I bought myself a gift. Something nice and expensive because I deserved it.

"I am my own Santa." Since that day, I have understood the meaning of "be your own Santa" and have continued to be my Santa. Some wonderful things have happened since:

1. Christmas is not on December 25th. **It is on any day I choose.**
2. **I celebrate when I want to,** for any reason that I want to.
3. Being Santa means that **I can change my mood any time** by gifting myself whatever it may be.

I know it sounds a bit selfish, but there is a deeper truth behind it. Unless you can be a Santa to yourself, you cannot be one to others. I am very sure that the real Santa Claus (I have never met him) surrounds himself with a whole lot of happiness, love and laughter before he gives it away to the wonderful little children.

This Christmas, while you spread joy and happiness to others by wishing them, writing cards, forwarding mails and buying presents, I would love it if you also discovered being your own Santa. For some of you who are parents, this should not be difficult at all because you already are the Santa for your children. The time has come to be your own as well. Give it a try.

Let me help you make the shift. Here are some gifts you can give yourself as Santa. Some are absolutely free.

o **Give yourself the gift of writing down your goals.** Hey Santa, do read them out to yourself every single day. You will truly be surprised before next Christmas. That is a promise.

- **Give yourself the gift of learning.** Gift yourself twelve books for the year and resolve to read and study one every month, also putting into practice what the books say.

- **Give yourself the gift of giving.** Unconditionally give gifts to those you love. Throw your reasons and conditions out the door (examples of conditions: "I will do it when…… [wait for some other event]" and "I will do it if he or she does"). Even if giving the gift stretches you a little extra, *do it*. There is magic in giving unconditionally. It comes back to you manifold in no time.

- **Give yourself the gift of something that will make you feel good.** It should be something nice, something that you have been wanting but not buying for yourself. It should be something fun, something that makes you smile. I like to gift myself something that looks good or feels good—a piece of art, a nice desk, a new camera, a holiday for no reason, a nice watch. If something makes you smile, others will smile when they see you. That is the spirit of Christmas that Santa likes to create! Doesn't he?

- **Be thankful.** Everyone must be thankful for something in life. Yes, we all have problems and probably count them every day, at home and at work. Count the things you are thankful for in life. Be your Santa and give yourself the gift of thankfulness. You will soon realize that the energy that thankfulness creates is a key to personal success.

Okay Santa, the challenge is yours. Put on the suit now and live it up because now is the best time and you deserve it.

Here is my favorite part—you will develop the passion and energy and discover your Santa any day you want to.

It is not just fun; it is the biggest tool you will ever find for building belief.

Go do it.

10
Ignore your Mother. Ignore Your Father.
Section 2: Breakthroughs

On a memory lane, three incidents occurred to me that led me to this writing.

The 1st one.

I was six. I don't remember exactly how, but I had found my way outside the house into this second hand Ambassador that my Dad had just bought. It was being cleaned. I sat inside to pretend drive. I was having fun. Suddenly I spotted the key hanging from the ignition switch and started to turn. Cars back then obviously cranked and didn't just start.

I could hear my Dad running down from the third floor, screaming, 'stop, stop, stop, stop'... What did I do... Crank Crank. Crank. Crrrrrrrannnnnnnnnkkkk.

It was fun. I don't remember getting yelled at. Though I am sure it happened. I purely remember an incident of pure joy and remember a six-year-old feeling like a man.

My Dad obviously couldn't bear the thought of me getting hurt. And I don't suggest that you don't stop your children when they do that. Just 'enjoy' it too when they just do it.

The 2nd one.

I was nine. Me and my friends around the neighborhood were in this cycling phase. All of us strictly instructed to stay within the confines of 'F' block (that's where I stayed). "No venturing out, its really dangerous. Bad things can happen," my mother would remind me some ten thousand times before I'd take the bike out.

This was August. Kite flying time in Delhi. Cycling was getting boring but we didn't have kites. We didn't have money to buy them either but that we'll only realize a little later. So what do we do to get kites? Lets break a little rule. Lets go beyond the 'F' block. Not just little beyond, we went about 10 miles in peak rush hour

Boy if was fun. No kites because no money. We at the time hated the shopkeeper for no just giving them. We loved our ride and the little race on the way back.

Problem? Got home too late.

Yelled at? You bet! My folks were horrified, scared and panicking. Obviously.

It was too good. I slept grinning from ear to ear.

The 3rd one.

I was 14. Four days back I had fractured my left wrist. A fresh plaster was sparkling white, shinning.

Five days back I had committed to playing Badminton match representing my local club. We used to do this often and take turns participating. Your turn came once in three months. So I wasn't going to miss it! After all I only need my right hand to play.

Dressed. Ready. And set to leave home. "NO WAY" - a stern "NO WAY" from both Mom and Dad. They just couldn't let me jerk and toss my fractured hand around fearing that I might hurt it more. I sulked. But half an hour later sneaked out on some excuse. Without rackets of course.

I played. Against all odds, I won. My first competition win ever. I was on top of the world. So happy that the eternal sin was committed - I walked home with my 'proud' cup in my hand.

Busted.
Scolded.
Grounded.

But very proud.

I took my shots. And I made it. And yes I loved it.

Why am I telling you these stories?

- **Often, your closest friends and family advise against taking our shots** - not in sports, per se, but in our business or our life. They do it to protect us. They warn us of what might not work with our new business plan. Or what could go wrong if we land that big interview. Or how risky it is to open your own restaurant or start your own business or just take up an alternate career.

- **They tell you they love you and that, "it's not you, it's the economy,"** or, "you're great but it's such a competitive industry." Your friends tell you about what can go wrong, but rarely about what can go right. It's because they don't want to see you get hurt. They love you so much that they rather see you achieve a 'lot less' than see you hurt.

Everyone relates to this. Right? We've all seen it. So what to do?

Two Choices.

- **One**

    Nothing.
    Give In.
    Be Safe.
    No hurt.

No pain.
You'll be fine.

o Two - This is what I'd want you to do....

Ignore them
Ignore you Mom.
Ignore your Dad.
Ignore your well-wishers.
Take the shot.
Take your shot.

And here are five reasons why I'd love you to do this;

1. **You will regret the things that you not do (the shots that you don't take) much more (MUCH MUCH MUCH MORE) than the shots that you missed.** Yes, it may temporarily please someone that you abode, though, the regret will eat you up over time.

2. As Wayne Gretzky tells us, **"You miss 100% of the shots you don't take."**

3. **If someone gives you advice, consider the source carefully.** Are your goals greater than the accomplishments of the source itself? If yes, erase the advice immediately and quickly.

4. When your friends and family help you choose between two alternatives, **they will most likely recommend that you choose the easier path. Don't do it.** Choose the harder one.

5. **Don't ask others for advice -- solicit insight.** BIG Difference. Only you can make the decision. Only you know what you are capable of. No one else.

Yes when you do this things can go wrong. And people will shout in your face 'I told you so'. My friend develop an attitude of **So What?**

You tried.
You fell flat.
Failed.
Loser.
Dejected.
'I told you so.'
'Its not for you'

Get up.
Ready again.
Aim. Fire.
Go for it.
Fall again.
Repeat.
Its your life. Not someone else's.
You have the right to fail.
And rise.
As many times as you want.

I live by this statement - **Life is about experiences and success. Not about perfection.**

I would love for you to try the same.

Start.
Go.
Shoot.
Leap.
Launch.
Fire.
Move.

Create.
Try.
Experiment.
Do.

Your mother, father (and your friends) will be right behind you. They love you. And then you'll be soaking up their words of encouragement and congratulations for your accomplishments. Allow them to tell you, "I always knew you will make it", then smile on. It's a great moment.

And then pass on the lesson the next generation.

11
The Winners Dozen
Section 2: Breakthroughs

Yes, you have seen plenty like this I assume.

I am not very keen on the word 'winner' - I think the concept and idea of winning is overrated, overused, over abused and has roots primarily in winning relatively. That is winning or performing better than someone else.

Even though this list is about winning, it is not about your concept of winning. It is not about coming 1st.

> Michael Jackson was #1. **Did he win?**

> Lance Armstrong, the undisputed hero!! - **Winner?**

Mulling over my experience of coaching people and consulting with organizations to generate breakthroughs, in the middle of the night, I put a small note into my iPhone -

Winning certainly is not coming 1st, neither it is the gold medal; Winning is not an aspiration. Winning is not in the future. Winning is the now, the next 5 minutes. Or not. Winning is a feeling. Winning is a constant presence, not an insecurity or an incompletion. You are either a winner or not, and that has nothing to do with the 1st position.

There is a very simple "are you a winner?" test - two questions -

1. Are you happy about everything you do and have in your life?

2. Do you always do the right thing or is it ok to sometimes compromise on values of integrity?

Of course you can lie to yourself and straight away answer a 'yes' to both and become a proven, certified loser anyway. The reason is simple - no one is happy (no one that you know) about EVERYTHING in life, by answering a yes (if you did) you already defied integrity.

Winners, as I know them, choose their attitude and the results follow. You see 'winning' is about being happy. Yet we aren't happy about everything. Herein comes integrity. The ability to acknowledge what isn't right. The winner fixes it, overcomes it and does the right thing because happiness matters. The losers live it because coming 1st or appearing good matters. Where are you? Are you acknowledging it?

So here it is. On these thoughts, I wrote a winners dozen. A list of daily attitude that it takes to be a winner, my kind of winner, not the #1 chasers but the ones who are chased by the #1.

1. **Your call and yours alone.** You choose the attitude you live with, no matter what the reality. Things can be horribly wrong at the moment or incredibly fascinating, attitude is a choice. This choice determines happiness, not the reality. This choice creates the next reality. (Positive, Enthusiastic regardless of the reality because whatever reality you are mulling over is the 'past' anyway)

2. **Each day presents on a silver platter thousands of opportunities to turn around your situation.** If your attitude is positive and enthusiastic, you'll spot them easily. If your attitude is 'blame and self-pity', you'll dismiss them even more easily. Choose.

3. **Do the right thing versus the acceptable thing.** You body, mind and emotions know, whether you acknowledge or not, when you defied integrity. You may temporarily win and celebrate, though can never feel happy.

4. **Listen Aggressively.** If at all you need to be aggressive about something in life, it must be listening. Pick a person you admire, idolize and want to be like, I'll guarantee you picked an aggressive listener. (Effective Listening is Effective Leadership).

5. **Cherish your failures.** I know this sounds preachy. I am a common sense person. See - failures will happen, right? Can't get everything right, can you? So when you know that they are going to happen, somewhere or the other, when you know they are almost unavoidable, then why choose a negative emotion over a positive one?

6. **Read. Or Learn (another way).** A new thing or thought. It always feels good to.

7. **Be nice. Always. No matter what.** Anger, resentment, outbursts (are reactions to past events and past is over) as emotions over calmness and composure (are preparations for future events) ruin your chances of spotting solutions.

8. **Help. Give. Make a Difference. Today. Now. Right Now.** We all look for reasons or events, when we'll do something for someone. Stop it. Stop operating selfishly. Make this a religion - that's a true winner - the ability to help, give and make a difference in another person's life unconditionally. Do it and see for yourself - there isn't another greater joy.

9. **Smile. There is always something to smile about.** Finding those things teaches you to choose positive emotions.

10. Arrive early. Leave later (outwork everyone. Old fashioned but works. Try it.)

11. **Talk, breathe, think and discuss solutions.** The world loves

to talk about problems and then blame everyone for them. The only way to train yourself to think about breakthroughs, the only way to be a real winner is to do the opposite - **think solutions.** All the time. You have moved from the past to the future.

12. (Repetition, because its so VERY IMP) **Happiness Always.** Happiness (Winning) is not an aspiration. Its now. **The next 5 minutes. Or Not. Never.**

12

How Do You Succeed

Section 2: Breakthroughs

THINK! - About the beliefs you have picked up all along these years, right from the time you understood a language to now.

Parents, teachers, friends, colleagues and others you spend your time with - their wisdom, their thoughts and their beliefs are and has been the foundation of your values, your attitudes, your believes, your personality, and your achievement.

In a nutshell, parents and siblings, friends and colleagues, shape your self-esteem.

To a great extent you learn about success, about the concept of how much to achieve, what is enough or what will never be enough, mostly from parents and siblings.

For a long time I found lots of things that could have been better in terms of belief systems I was passed on.

Like it or not, their lessons (even the ones you hated), whether you rejected them or embraced them have been burnt into our brains and psyche. It guides our life. Unknowingly we all emulate.

For a long time I focused on 'what could have been'… but then I learnt an amazing thing – I learned to filter the great from the good and the good from the not so good.

Once I understood the impact of this on our achievements, I realized how much we could self-destruct by focusing on what's not there. The search into my lessons learnt from my parents and siblings led me to understand a few principles that shape success (at least mine).

I'll lead you on, perhaps you'll know what I mean or what I desire for you to do.
My mother told me over and over as a kid whenever there would

be tears, "Get rough. Get tough!" And I have always followed that philosophy of, "Get back up, find another way and get on with it."

'My father was one of extreme logic, "The secret to deal with increased expenses: earn more money."

Many of my role models, my learning mates are alive, but I haven't met them. They're not necessarily role models for who they are. In most cases I don't even know who they are or how they led their lives.

Yet they are for what they do or rather from whatever I read what I interpreted it to be – the learning deciphered.

Sachin Tendulkar and Steve Jobs are at the top of the list. My close friends are up there too.

My writings (including the inspiration to write this one), are almost always born out of these ideas and what I learned or sparked off from one of them.

I'm passing the condensed version of that wisdom on to you and hoping that you would endeavor to discover your own too.

There are many teachings that have inspired. Inspired in business, in writing and in living.

Here are a few timeless ones'

- **A way to life – Christpher Logue**

    Come to the edge.
    We might fall.
    Come to the edge.

It's too high!
COME TO THE EDGE!
And they came,
and we pushed,
And they flew.

- **Napolean Hill (attitude and goals)** - Action is the real measure of intelligence.

- **Groucho Marx (humor)** - I find television very educating. Every time somebody turns on the set, I go into the other room and read a book.

- **A book I read in when I was 15** - Don't remember the book but made a note after reading it.

  If you want to be free, then live. If you simply want a life, then abide.

- **Rig Veda (truth)-** Desire links non-being to being.

- **My recent studies into the subject of self esteem-**

  Self-esteem (the only determinant of achievement) is directly proportionate to integrity. Whenever you stand by your word, the self-esteem goes up. Whenever you falter on your word, self-esteem goes down. Truth. Period.

- **Ayn Rand (writing style and philosophy)-**

  Government "help" to business is just as disastrous as government persecution. The only way a government can be of service to national prosperity is by keeping its hands off.
- **Dale Carnegie (making friends and public speaking).**

You can close more business in two months by becoming interested in other people than you can in two years by trying to get people interested in you.

- **Margaret Fuller (substance)- Today a reader, tomorrow a leader.**

- **Benjamin Franklin-** Energy and Persistence conquer all things.

- **Earl Pertnoy (life's lessons)-** Antennas up!

- **Budha (wisdom)-** However many holy words you read, however many you speak, what good will they do you if you do not act on upon them?

These people have passed on but their teachings are immense. It's a whole belief system by itself. Beliefs are wonderful. Though actions produce results.

Figure out where your beliefs lie. Are they laying low in the 'disempowering truths' we all heard from our parents and teachers? There is an easy way to find out – Are you acting on what you really, truly would love to achieve or be, whatever that may be – in terms of health or wealth or - if the answer is a murmured 'no', then you know what beliefs rule over you.

Listen, pay attention, observe, and study. Do all of what you do but figure out the beliefs that you go by and ACT.

'Mindlessly work on what life has thrown at you' was never my motto and never will be.

One life to live and it isn't coming back is my truth, my motivation…

What's yours?
Who teaches you?
Who inspires you?
Who helps you achieve?

13

This Is (or should be) Management
Section 3: Management

Get Over The Theories Of Management and Leadership that someone at Harvard wrote in the '50's and every other B-School (abbreviation BS) derived their curriculum from it.

Here are 40 Common (really uncommon in practice) Sense – Real World – Management. Get On Board or Off Business.

1. **Stop Seeking The Best Talent.** Check Your Definition Of Best Talent. It is not the smartest that reached the tip of the Everest. It is the one with oodles of passion combined with good old-fashioned hard work. Hard Work beats Smart Work most of the times.

2. **GUTS!!** – Someone who doesn't have the guts to say "You are wrong, Boss" is of ZERO value. Bosses who have subordinates who don't disagree with them are of NEGATIVE value.

3. **Hire Disrespectful People** who question authority and challenge everything.

4. The Mavericks, The Big Breakthrough Producers were all **Messy, Disorganized, Rude, People**.

5. **Breakthrough is in the Market** - not at your Desk.

6. **Forget Built to Last and forget Good to Great.** Its plain theory. Change, Leading Change internally and externally is the only game.

7. **BIG wouldn't survive.** Keep breaking it.

8. **Continuous Improvements (KAIZEN) and Six Sigma are innovation killers.** Look what it has done to its inventor – Motorola.

9. **STOP IT> FORGET IT>** The modern management challenge is to stop being busy. Do nothing. Forget and unlearn a LOT MORE that you learn.

10. Breakthroughs are very easy. **Its blocked by the BOSS most often.**

11. **How enthusiastic and energy attracting is your senior management?** Couldn't answer a loud YES? – Ah! Went after the boring best talent, didn't you?

12. Your **Brand Inside is far more important than your Brand Outside.**

13. Action Is More Important than Your Strategy Retreat. **Do now. Think Later.**

14. 50% of your decisions will be wrong even if you spend 50% of your life in preventing the mistake. Keep Moving. **50% is good enough.** Stop wasting time in over analyzing.

15. **DON'T REWARD Mediocre Successes.** It will bring down your entire system to a minimum performance.

16. David Kelley: **"Fail Faster. Succeed sooner."**

17. **No One in your OFFICE has 8 hours of work.** Staring at computer is the biggest give-away for that. Make Market Visits Compulsory For ALL.

18. Hire People who had the **GUTS to not go after just academic education and** chose experiences instead. They have BELIEF!

19. **Hire Women in senior managements.** Transformation guaranteed.

20. Your business has to be in the Business of selling experience. **Fire everyone who talks about merely quality and satisfaction.**

21. **Don't make it the Best. Differentiate.** HINT: You don't buy the most durable, fall resistant, longest battery life, mobile phone. Do you? You buy the one that's cool and different. So why do you think the market will decide any differently?

22. If the average age of your Board is over 50 – they are **30 years behind.** God help you.

23. When you fail to reach your targets or goals for a year – Raise them further high. **Don't adjust to mediocrity.** Push them further so you are forced to innovate! –

    "The greatest danger for most of us is not that our aim is too high and we miss it, but that it is too low and we reach it." - Michelangelo.

24. When you fail to reach your targets or goals for a year – Raise them further high. **Don't adjust to mediocrity.** Push them further so you are forced to innovate! –

25. **Crush** Bureaucracy. **Crush** Politics. **Cut** Structures. **Cut** Designations. **Cut** Management Layers - every year as a part of growth. Flat structures OUTGROW layered structures without fail.

26. ERP Systems. I have yet to meet a company where it has made them more agile. **Herd mentality.**

27. **Break** dress codes. **Break** office timings. **Break** whatever. But disrupt, unsettle, change thinking, change patterns, change, change, change. You want people and processes to change. Managing the same thing year after year is not management, it's a comfortable, predictable, boring job.

28. What is going to be **RADICALLY DIFFERENT** about you this year. If nothing, then stop expecting different results.

29. **Think Gandhi** – No one gives you power. You take it.

30. Think **FUN**. People spend 50% of their lives at office. If they aren't having Fun, your Balance Sheet is just BS or will be soon.

31. Your Core Work Values will translate into behavior ONLY if you hold the values of **Honesty and Integrity** as number one (NO COMPROMISE AT ALL) – otherwise you may as well **trash the 'values' document.** That's what people do anyway.

32. **Meetings beyond 45 minutes often have no value.** You are setting the precedent for slow and painful and expecting results fast and plentiful. Ya right!

33. **THE ONLY WAY TO SHOW YOU CARE** – is to give your time to those you say you care about…. People are not dumb – they know difference between words and actions.

34. **SUCCESS = SALES. Period**. Sales = Customers. Period. Is every function focused outward? If not, you are losing sales.

Period.

35. If the Boss knows everything and never says "I don't know" – then no one else is exploring. **This Boss Wont Grow Your Company.**

36. **Speed over Accuracy** will win you more games.

37. **People do not resist change.** It will take however long to change as you think it will.

38. **The biggest motivator is appreciation.** That's also the fastest way to bring about change.

39. And again – Integrity = **Success.** Integrity = **Speed.** Integrity = **Power.**

40. **Performance Appraisal** is an opportunity to praise people. Not for what you use it.

    And Last – For God's Sake – **Don't call Humans, Resources.** HR is a sick terminology. Pause and think for a moment, you'll realize, it is sick. Call them humans and treat them humanly.

14
The Great Management Bullshit
Section 3: Management

This is not meant to degrade or look down upon what managements do. I respect the success it has brought us over the years. However, this is certainly meant to point out practices and policies that we are following without ever pausing to think - 'why?'

If you are looking to survive and be moderately successful, this is not for you, you are fine the way you are. If you are looking to **breakthrough the convention** and do something spectacular, this list of (non)wisdom is certainly for you.

Here It Is. in no particular order.

BS-1- The Boardroom. Boardroom Strategy is Bored-Room Strategy. Business is not a dry, dreary, numbers affair. It is about emotions and adventures. People with real, true, to die for, passions climb mountains. The others keep making glamorous plans in the comfort of their rooms.

Which one is your organization - the glamorous planners or the gritty doers?

Who do you think will produce the spectacular?

BS-2- Efficiency & Excellence. Efficiency and Excellence is not the goal of your business.

Long ago, to ease the pressure on management, the company was divided (or organized) into a structure - sales, marketing, operations, finance, production and so on.

The goal of any business (in reality, no matter what your vision document says) is to make money or profit or growth or scale.

The goal of the structures that you divided the business into is not that. It is to be the best - the most efficient.

The management assumes that if these structures are most efficient individually, then collectively the business will be too.

That is simply untrue. Its BS. Here's why.

In being individually efficient, you miss out in making the other one efficient, that is you miss out on interdependence, that is you miss out to make the business efficient, that is you miss out doing the right thing for the business. Yes you do the right thing for the department and achieve the highest efficiency. So what, is that the goal?

BS-3- Experienced People. What is the role of experience? Do you know?

Here is what experience does. It provides you with a solution based on the norm. It provides wisdom based on past experience. Right?

By this logic, it also denies you a solution against the norm that is it kills innovation.

Does your culture permit to challenge (threadbare challenge) authority? If not, you don't have a hope for innovation.

Yes experience is needed. It provides the business stability so it doesn't have to reinvent everyday though if experience breeds conformity (as it does in most institutions), you will remain mediocre, as do most institutions.

BS-4- Lets get organized, planned and structured. Chaos > Organized.

Before anything can get structured, the breakthrough is always in the chaos. NOTE: There is no breakthrough that I have studied that wasn't in some way a result of the chaos around it. Please also note, I am not saying undisciplined, I am saying unorganized.

Don't box people into tight organized structures, then run around the organization screaming at them to 'think out of the box'. How crazy is that?

Breakthroughs depend on those leaders who cherish the mess.

BS-5- Performance Management System. Your Performance Management System, really is PMS (literally)

Performance Management Systems build on *Key Result Areas* to produce efficiency and measure it, is worthless. Unless you can think of a way to measure ROI or Impact on Profit, you have in reality absolutely no clue on why you are measuring what you are. It just causes stress for everyone - the one who manages and the one who is being managed.

And answer this - A system that causes stress, what will it produce?

BS-6- Lets become Big - And get into one Big Office. Big Stinks (mostly)

Upstairs become establishments and then gets constantly attacked by next round of upstairs. Big Company performance has and always will be more problematic than imagined. No matter what you think, as long as an upstairs is available, consulting them on decisions becomes mandatory. That is, it kills agility, empowerment and spontaneity. Unless you are constantly breaking it, you are no doing your job as management.

BS-7- Kaizen, TQM, and other Jargons! Dangerous Stuff!

Brilliant ideas. Yes. They were brilliant for the time and in the time that they solved the problems of that time.

Look, pause, and think - Perfection gets in the way of the next big thing. The next big thing as may be conceived by the weirdo in your company will never be perfect. If you make it perfect, you will kill it.

The sole survivor in Forbes List of Giants from 1917 to the list in 2003 is GE. All on the list used these tools. So what went wrong?

They are excellent tools. So what? Just because you have an excellent quality tool lying around at you plant or in your garage, does it mean you start repairing your plant and your car?

Wisdom?

BS-8- Sustainability. Destruction Rules!

Change the world? Yes
Dream big? Yes
Aim for the skies? Absolutely

Whether your change will still be leading the world in 2075? Who cares!
Permanence is a delusion. Build To Last is a foolish idea.

You want your company to last. You have to accept the words, 'Keep Changing'. Settling and Sustaining is for and in the grave or in the museum.

Put all your energies into surviving todays Tsunamis of change. Let the day after tomorrow define the next change. If you put energies into protecting your earlier change so that it sustains, you will obviously be out-run.

BS-9- The Best Talent. What are you building, a business or a CV?

You don't need to mindlessly chase best talent (a Grade Business School, abbreviated as **A Grade BS**) to build a great business. You need people who will do the tasks that are needed to be done.

What are these tasks? Which task is making the business underperform? Which task is pulling the entire system down? Putting people (no matter from which Biz School) into any other task is going to have ZERO impact on your success.

BS-10- Its just a perception. Perception is all that there is.

I recently attended a Boardroom presentation of one of the largest Indian companies. A 25-year experienced company veteran was glowing with excitement at presenting his new supply chain initiative. The board gleaming obviously because they sanctioned the budgets. They barely noticed that I had dozed off in the middle of this grand recitation. When I was asked for my comments, I trashed it with a simple question - How is this adding to your profits? The two hour debate that followed was on how it is a never before done innovation. How does it add to profits? Conclusion - It doesn't. Further conclusion - Trash it.

You see, the presentation was fine. The idea was foolish. The idea was based on 25 years of perception based on internal realities. My feedback was based on exposure to external realities.

Think about it. Are you really as 'far out' as you think you are.

BS-11- Haste Makes Waste. Yes. So go waste. What's the

problem?

From all of life's experience, any entrepreneur will tell you that failure is the mother (father, uncle, sister, brother.....) of success.

Yet when it comes to managing their organizations, the one thing that managements resist the most is failure!! Wonder!

Not that I am saying that you take big risks and fall flat on your face. That won't happen. Your board will take care of that.
Though if you're demolishing an executive because he failed, you are killing the success to follow. You are not doing the company any favor.

Think about it - when your kid failed at walking at the first attempt, what did you do? You encouraged and clapped and eventually he or she took the first step. It was joyous, wasn't it?

What do you do now, when he or she fails, will largely decide whether you are accepted or detested.

Which one of these qualities (accepted or detested), will your people turnaround for?

BS-12- Commit to the target. Commit to the target. Say a loud YES. Screw Ups are the real mark of Excellence.

Walmart CEO David Galss summed up a single trait of founder Sam Walton's success. He said, 'Sam is not afraid to fail. His attitude is that we Got That Dumb One Behind Us, now lets try something else. Right now.'

What are you doing? Are you admonishing people when they miss or are you finding ways of doing something else?

Yes you chase bold targets but by definition bold targets have an element of misses. People missed, so what? Remember BS-11- Failure is the mother of success, unless of course you kill the son.

BS-13- Behave like a leader should. The noisiest classroom wins the gold in reality.

Read this and weep profusely. From Jordan Ayan's book *Aha*. "My wife and I went to a parent-teacher (kindergarten) conference. Our budding child got a grade 'Unsatisfactory' in art. We were shocked. How could anyone get a grade like that at such a young age? His teacher informed us that he refused to 'color within the lines', which is a state requirement for demonstrating 'grade-level motor skills.' "

Our school systems are crafted to deliver A-GRADE CONFORMISTS. Our management systems run by people out of these schools, are naturally then crafted to look down upon the non-conformists.

If everyone starts conforming to your belief systems and not make noise – then you will produce no Roger Bannister, no Edison, no Steve Jobs, and no breakthrough.

You don't want cubicle slaves, do you?

Tomorrow's Requirement No.1 – In business and In Parliament - **Kids who color outside the lines.**

BS-14- Not A job for HER. SHE is the Best Leader.

Break that mindset. Its stupid. I am not some pro-women liberalization movement leader. I am talking form logic.

Women naturally link rather than rank workers. Judy Rossener researched this in her book.

A BusinessWeek special report based on engagement studies in 2000 organizations conclude: "As leaders, women rule. People interviewed submit that women managers outshine their male counterparts in almost every measure."

BS-15- Customer Satisfaction and Quality. Junk it. Its old school.

Experiences and Solutions today trump satisfaction and quality.

And This is a Big Deal. One fall and the iPhone shatters (yes I am a living owner of a broken one). Its not durable. Defies quality to that extent. Does it mean I am going to replace it with a sturdy hard-rock durable, high quality, better battery phone? Not a chance!

But why?

Bottom-line. For the time being. Apple is a better experience. A better solution.

What are you selling?

Are you sweating over satisfaction and quality still? That is a given in todays world.

Think experience and engagement or think winding up.

BS-16- Let's Build Consensus. Majority Opinions are Mostly Wrong!

Why do you need to build consensus? So that the execution flows through, right?

Here's the deal.

Success of any change depends on two things: 1- Do people believe that the proposed change is good for them? and 2- Does the change deliver immediate and excellent results for everyone?

If these two are taken care of (let me tell you, most cases they aren't), that's all you need.

In building consensus, or aligning majority opinions, you lose the right solution. The majority in any given situation, tends to conform to the least conflicting path and not necessarily to the right path. Also majority always aligns to the path of least resistance (that is the most secured option). Again not necessarily the right path.

If majority opinions were right, you and I would be in love with our politicians!

Its rarely ever right. Where are your mavericks? Find them and deal with change the way it should be dealt with - with results.

BS-17- Corporate Leadership Team. What is their role?

Management has a lot to do with answers. Leadership is purely a function of questions. There in lies a conflict!

Leadership is about 'creating a cause' for others so they will passionately follow. Management is about 'giving direction' to others so they will execute. Are your leaders doing the managers job? If yes (mostly it s always Yes), then both the leaders as well as the managers are not doing their jobs.
The Corporate Leadership Team or The Senior Leadership Team or

The Board Whatever Team.... no matter what fancy term you follow.... ends up giving direction to the subsequent levels on what to do. That by function is not their job.

The leaders' job is simply this - **to create leaders**. That doesn't happen through managing. It does through challenging. It doesn't happen through answering, it happen through questioning. It doesn't happen through managing (obviously), it happens through leading!

Serious Suggestion: Include 20-year olds in your leadership teams who will ask embarrassing but fundamental questions.

BS-18- I sent a mail. Crappy X Functional Communication Is THE Major Issue.

When email becomes an excuse (or a cc too), rather than genuine communication, you know you have lost the plot. There are two things that have happened because of email that is leading to the lowest standard of cross-functional relations:

1. You will rather communicate on the mail than walk a few meters down the hall and talk in person. This is a sign of a highly (MOST HIGHLY) **unassertive behavior.** Really, really stinks!

2. In the earlier days, when email wasn't there - **from time to thinking till time to communicating - had a delay. The moment passed.** One rationalized it before speaking it. Many a times realized that the communication itself wasn't needed.

Today that delay of gratification doesn't happen.

BS-19- Let's put a System. Please systemize the process of (un)Dumbing

Systems provide rules. Rules needed for processing information and channelizing it appropriately. This is fine.

When was the last time you checked whether your systems are helping you or un-helping you?

I'll give you an example. Most companies fall into the lure of developing systems (popularly called ERPs) to meet their New Scale. Very soon you also realize that the very own systems sap (pun intended!) the very spirit of the enterprise!

Very soon you also realize that it might not have been the right solution. So you pump more modules into it to justify what, a wrong system!!

Very soon it occurs, though you never realize, that you basically dumped your money. But you go on justifying it (because in all your presentations you have blown your trumpet so much) by dumping even more of it.

Most of the work your system is handling, common sense could have handled better. Have a system if you may, please create an anti-system System too, so you now when its started becoming dumb.

BS-20- People Resist Change. You DON'T KNOW the change!

Change, too is a state of mind.
People don't resist change. And here's proof.

Supposing your boss gives you a 10 Million Dollar bonus tomorrow. Will you say 'No' to it?

Why not?

Its going to change your life! how come you aren't resisting it. People do not resist change. **They examine whether the change is good for them or not and decide whether to go along with it or not.**

This basically means that they don't believe you when you say its good and that's not their fault.

BS-21- Change Initiatives Takes Time. What Clock Are You Using?

Change takes a minute, if that. No kidding!

Its been argued in many journals that AA (Alcohol Anonymous) is the most effective change program ever. Do you know how long does it take to stop drinking? One second and then the hard work begins.

It takes a second to change. That's it. No matter what the change. You (and I can prove this, statistically) are not implementing the change because you haven't a clue on what you will do post introducing the change. Going on preparing people for that change isn't the solution - Ensuring a win for all post change, is the solution.

It doesn't take time, again it takes thought! and that might be resisted forever!

BS-22- I don't have the time, Lets do it tomorrow! If you care, you are there

"My calendar is blocked, why don't you manage it, you have my support."

Ever used this line?

Bix Bender sums up this behavior beautifully. He says, "You can pretend to care. You cannot pretend to be there."

Being there matters. Or it won't get done. Not being there tells people - its not serious enough. Period.

BS-23- Huddle room. Lets Brainstorm. Why can't you not know when that is the truth.

I love the term, 'I don't know' because that is one term that means exactly what it says - that I don't know.

You know what true empowerment is - the words 'I don't know' - true empowerment is making people think, not making them think on what you are thinking - but making them think on what they will think.

Think!!!!

BS-24- Rewards for Success. And for Failures?

Mediocre successes are a tragic waste. Mediocre successes getting rewarded lay the foundation for the organization to systemize the tragic waste.

You see people say that they want recruits with spotless records. I say that spots are what matter most. The spotless will probably deliver you a good job, a current growth rate. Its the spot that will deliver you the breakthrough.

The quiet humble leaders (as Jim Collins will describe in 'Good to Great') will give you stability, yes no doubt about that.

Though, the bold, brash, egocentric dreamer will dent the universe (for example Steve Jobs, and he will never make it to Jim's list).

If you don't know how to nurture failure, you will be consistently mediocre.

BS-25- Continuous Improvements. BOLD LEAPS?

One thing I do agree with Good To Great is this - Good is the enemy of great.

There is a big misconception. That to take Giant Leaps of success you need Big Resources and Bigger Risks and so the better route will be continuous improvement.

You don't need bigger risks. You need a change of thinking. A change of rules. A change of assumptions.

You don't know yet how to do it, you could get in touch and we'll pass you case studies of where its been done.

BS-26- Values. There is only one check. Integrity.

If you have integrity and honesty engrained in your system, you don't need to document any values at all. They all flow.

If you have documented your values and 'integrity' explicitly stated is not on that list - you have failed. Don't launch any programs. They will eventually fail too.

You think you will tolerate a country (your country) in the long term if it lacks integrity. Would you?

If not, why would employees tolerate a company like that?

Shying away from living 'honesty and integrity' as a number-1 value basically indicates you are a crook. That's the message it sends to people, to your ecosystem. Eventually, the crooks get found out. Beware!!

BS-27- The Numbers Game
People Is The Game

The Best Plans Wins - is the era of MBAs.

In our research we have found something else. Firms that honored commitments made to their employees, delighted in the provision of service to them, cherished internal entrepreneurs and followed principles of integrity - YES - have outperformed all others by 10 is to 1 in its 'longevity' of profitable existence. The rest is or will be history soon.

BS-28- Economy Is Looking Gloomy. Try Enthusiasm!

If you have like a 70% market share and the economy stagnates, yes may be you have a worry or two.

If you don't have that kind of a market share, then basically you don't have any sensible competitive advantage. And you go on blaming the economy for that. Attack the problem. Spare the economy.

Here's the message:

Enthusiasm begets Enthusiasm.
Clouds (over economy) beget gloom (over business).
'Attack the problem' begets the solution.
'Attack the economy' begets helplessness.
People who have given up see it as half empty.

Winners see it as half full.
Hope begets hope.

You knew this all, already and still blame the economy?

Who said knowledge is good enough?

BS-29- Meetings... Meetings.... More Meetings.... Fun Is Not a Four-Letter Word.

I was conducting a seminar for students. I advised them ,"Never go to a place where laughter is not the norm"

The thing about learning is that it does not occur in a classroom. It occurs outside when you play with knowledge. That's my grouse against excessive meetings, no learning occurs in your meeting room, it occurs outside.

Unless there is 'fun' outside, that learning will become boring. If it becomes boring, it won't reoccur.

Laughter is not about cracking stupid jokes. Its about building a culture where people are happy. Right?

Take a poll of people exiting meeting rooms in your company tomorrow. You'll get a barometer on happiness quotient that will break the needle on the negative incline! Guaranteed.

BS-30- Topline. Bottom-line. Growth Rate. Numbers. What About The Amazing Grace

I don't disagree with numbers. A business wouldn't exist if it stopped making profits. So yes it is absolutely essential. But do we over do it? Perhaps, yes, because as I wander around companies and their corridors, I do realize that **'Grace' is a word lost and forgotten.**

I love 'grace'.

There is almost no discussion of 'grace' in the management books or for that matter in your hallways. And yet you, the business and I cannot exist without 'grace'.

Enterprises exist to serve. To serve customers and to serve employees. To serve communities and to serve shareholders.

Service is an act of grace. You forget 'grace' and you will forget why your enterprise exists. And soon forget existence too. Logical, isn't it? **Does Grace have any place in business, in our cutthroat competitive environment?**

Foolish question.

Of course it does.

Don't believe me? Lose it and find out what happens!

15

CEOs Are Idiots When
Section 3: Management

I was in Dubai sometime back. I faced a few sticky situations. I am generally polite. In these stuck situations, I met a lot of common sense defying people. It was frustrating.

On the way back, I began thinking of common sense defying stuff that we do.

So politely putting, I am not suggesting that CEOs are idiots. For the sake of making this interesting, I am suggesting that the following is idiotic and defies common logic. It is when they do the following that they are indeed idiots. Not you, of course!

In summary, CEOs are Idiots when

1. **OVERestimate** their importance. **OVERestimate** their relevance. **UNDERestimate** how inconsequential they really are.

2. **Fail to spend hyper aggressively on Human Development.** They say people are their biggest assets. And then first up cut spending budgets on the welfare and development of their biggest assets. Smart eh!

3. **Manage the system through financial controls.** 'Management by values' far outperforms 'Management by Economics'.

4. **Hire MBAs in large numbers.** Seriously, Masters of **Administration**!... How many administrators do you need? And why?

5. **Recruit mostly from traditional resources and then wonder why 'herd' mentality exists.**

6. **Don't invest in the real risk-takers and freaks.**

7. **Worry too much about Benchmarking, Improvements and other consulting jargons.** Not enough about Disruption and Innovation.

8. **Think Processes. Process. Process. Process.** Hello CEO, you are working with human beings. In our world, Passion beats process.

9. **Spends all his or her time in office. Not in the field.** Staying in office is basically choosing to deal with secretarial gossip handling over real world challenges. Come on.

10. **ARE NOT LOVED by the front line customer facing staff!**

11. **Don't have women in the executive team.** Women leaders are outperforming male counterparts world over. Wake up.

12. **Don't have enough cultural diversity in the executive team.** Prone to single-minded thinking to justify thought process.

13. **Advisors = BHOs (by hierarchy only).** Not accessible to juniors with a crazy thought process. That's a sign of becoming old (not in age, in the mind).

14. **Uses management lingo!** for example 'we greatly appreciate your results........' versus the inspiring Technicolor language - 'Wow! I love what you did today'

15. **COMMUNICATES MORE ON EMAIL LESS IN PERSON.**

16. **Holds reviews to discuss numbers and correct flaws.** Ever

heard of 'acknowledgement'. Now here is a psychology thing that works, really does - A behavior acknowledged is a behavior repeated. You want results - you acknowledge results. Conversely, you unknowingly and constantly acknowledge the presence of flaws and failures - What do you think you get the next time?

17. **Rewards mediocre successes and punishes excellent failures.** Needs to be reversed - CELEBRATE excellent failures and not the mediocre successes.

18. **Focused on Short-Term Quarter to Quarter Earnings rather than building a Long-Term Fun and Passion filled place.**

19. **Most Idiotic is this.** When Dreams = Bigger Market Share. Get Bigger. Cut Costs. What sort of a dream is that?

    How many people does it inspire? When you day dream about your life and find yourself quietly smiling away in a corner, have you ever smiled about market shares and costs?

    If a CEO FAILS TO INSPIRE ME BY THE AUDACITY OF THEIR DREAMS, HE WILL OR HAS FAILED. PERIOD.

So here it is.

As I said very politely in Dubai to each act of common sense defiance: "Thank you very much", I say very politely to the CEOs offended by this that 'I am sorry that CEOs are idiots'. Sorry 19 times over.

16
Culture Of Sustainable Entrepreneurship
Section 3: Management

"Lets create Entrepreneurial thinking in our organization."

This is a very popular buzzword in modern day boardrooms. The intent of entrepreneurism is wonderful. As was revealed to us, it is inspired by businesses and teams promising to but not reaching their stated goals.

The assumption that managements make is that entrepreneurial mindset may well be the answer.

But do they understand entrepreneurial thinking? Do they know what it means? If people had that mindset, wouldn't they be entrepreneurs? Do they know how to develop this thinking? Is asking Human Resources to do some programs going to be enough? Where should they begin?

Here is a brief summary of what it takes

1. **Genetically disposed to Innovations that upset apple carts** (3M Apple, FedEx, Virgin)

    Message: Innovate or Perish. Build to Innovate.

2. **Perpetually determined to outdo oneself, even to the detriment of today's $$$ winners (Apple, Microsoft, Amazon)**

    Message: Change begins within. It begins proactively. It means letting go.

3. **Love the Great Leap / Enjoy the Hunt** (Apple, Oracle, Intel)

    Message: Are your people enjoying the pursuit? Really tough one!

4. **Culture of Outspoken-ness** (Intel, Microsoft, FedEx,

CitiGroup, PepsiCo)

Message: Are your leaders challenged every day? If not, it's not entrepreneurial.

5. **Encourage Vigorous Dissent/ Genetically "Noisy"** (Intel, Apple, Microsoft)

   Message: Are you listening?

6. **"Culturally" as well as organizationally decentralized** (GE, J & J)

   Message: Power centered or Power De-centered?

7. **Multi-entrepreneurship / Many Independent-minded Stars** (GE, Time Warner)

   Message: The culture throws up the stars. The culture also swallows stars. Which one are you?

8. **Scour the world for Ingenious Alliance Partners—especially exciting start-ups** (Pfizer)

   Message: the established ones don't shift the market shares. Go for the challengers.

9. **Don't overdo "pursuit of synergy" - Do the right thing anyhow** (GE, J & J, Time Warner)
   Message: When you're doing the right thing, you don't need consensus.

10. **Find and Encourage and Promote Strong-willed/ Independent people** (GE, PepsiCo)

Message: Companies often lose these kinds of people and get stuck with the conformists.

11. **Ferret out Talent - anywhere and everywhere/ -"No limits" approach to retaining top talent** (Nike, Virgin, GE, PepsiCo)

    Message: Whatever it takes.

12. **The Star CEO is useless. The company should make him or her a star** (GE, PepsiCo....)

    Message: Latest Research - Star CEO effect to bottom-line - .016% worldwide.

13. **Up or Out** (GE, McKinsey, big consultancies and law firms and ad agencies and movie studios in general)

    Message: I am not a fan of Hire & Fire. Neither Am I a fan of living out mistakes. If you've made one. Correct it.

14. **Competitive to a fault!** (GE, Apple, News Corp/Fox, PepsiCo)

    Message: Competition isn't about win-lose. Its about the spirit. Play the game.

15. **Masters of Loose-Tight/Hard-nosed about a very few Core Values, Open-minded about everything else** (Virgin)

    Message: How open your organization is will determine how much it will experience.

17

Innovate Or Perish

Section 4: Innovation & Change

Growth. Sustainability. Scalability. What are you chasing?

Whatever be your challenge - a culture of 'innovation' covers it 'all'.

I read a book 'principles of innovation' - but innovation, can it have principles?

And so I started writing my own list of tactics for innovation. A list that I believe is imperative **(IMPERATIVE)** to creating a consistently innovative organization. This is about building an overall mechanism and culture for innovation. You might use some and you might discard some. I'll tell you one thing that a culture of innovation, a culture of shocking the world will be built by using them all. The absence of any of the following, weakens the others and kills the culture.

Use this as you may.

Do.Do.Do. Now. Fast. Make Mistakes. Fast. Do. Again. Fast.

1. **He who tries more stuff - wins.** An unbelievable fact - Innovation is a numbers game.

2. **The Try It NOW Culture - Emphasis on effort.** Try now, talk later. "We'll talk when we got something to show, but till then we'll keep trying."

3. **Failure celebrated.** Fast failure, rather discovery and acceptance of fast failure is key to innovation. Fast failure is key to fast turnaround is key to fast success. Period.

4. **No walls. No barriers. No secretaries. No floors. No corner offices.** Communication and accessibility must be as easy and welcome as breathing.

5. **Culture of 'not at desk' but 'wandering around'** Innovation is about spontaneity. And spontaneous ideas don't pop out of the computer screen.

6. **Speed of decision-making and implementation.** That is trying. Speed is key to sustaining an innovation culture. Nothing discourages an innovator more than procrastination.

7. **At your annual retreat have an award for the most valuable screw-up** so that people know its ok to fail as long as you try.

8. **Be LEAN.** More the designations and layers of management = Less the innovations. 100% of the time.

Discipline

9. **Innovation is not 'lets all have a blast'** - Dreaming with a deadline and budgeting till the milestone is as important to the culture to sustain innovation. Can't just be a freak-show.

10. Yes, screwing-up is essential for innovation but the **thinker must take responsibility for screwing-up,** capture learning and back to action. Fast. It is not the screwing up that should trouble you as management. Its the blaming you should address at the first sign of appearance. Kill it.

11. **Change the name of your senior management team to the team of execution** and redefine expectations to one word - Execution.

Its a Body Of People

12. **We are whom we exist with. Are their weird, crazy, mad people around?** If not, then you guys hanging out with each

other talking politics, cricket and org gossip will not be innovation anytime during your lifetime. Get people to hang around the right people. MOST IMPORTANT.

13. **Simple rule. Hang out with the challengers - Get challenged.** Hang out with the dull and boring - get dull and boring.

14. **Customers everywhere.** You are innovating for them, right? Customers at meetings, team meetings, awards, project teams. Everywhere.

15. **Benchmark carefully and insanely. Shift the lens.** You benchmark within the industry, you will worry about being 10% better. That will not lead to innovation that may lead to better management. Benchmark with landing the man on moon and create an equivalent, now we're talking!

16. **Breakthroughs of the world are occurring outside your corner office.** Company HO is unimportant. As hard as it may be for you to believe, for those at HO, please get out of there.

17. **Types of consultants you engage will influence how you approach problems.** If you are stuck with the big four, you are stuck with the problems of everyone in your industry. Rethink.

18. **Invest in building a knowledge network.** Become a university. Make it fast. Make it fun. Research. Document. Teach. Learn. Unlearn.

19. **Don't waste your lunch.** Lunch is 5 opportunities a week and 220 opportunities a year. Lunch with customers, vendors, people from other departments, frontline staff.

20. **Don't waste your meetings.** Most likely most of your time goes in meetings. Don't waste meetings. Invite crazy outside perspectives to every meeting. Get challenged.

HR = Supercool

21. **Hire Enthusiasm.** Staff, management or partners, hire enthusiasm. Throw the CV - Get to the heart. Enthusiasts are almost a synonym for innovators. Or at least the non-enthusiasts are guaranteed to not innovate.

22. **Young = Tomorrow. Old = Yesterday.** Are there exceptions to the rule? Sure. But not many. Dig deep for key promotions.

23. **Promote enthusiasm.** Enthusiasm as bosses is a no brainer. Beware enthusiasm is not equal to mindless extroversion. Enthusiasm can be silent too. But you'll know it when you see it.

24. **How do you measure performance? Are efforts given consideration or is it just the growth?** This one parameter will determine whether employees will try for 'new' or settle to give you the 'old'.

25. **Once an innovator, always an innovator.** Simple test. See what all your candidate has done, experimented, tried, failed at and experimented again. A usually 'sexy' resume doesn't have all this.

26. **Incentive schemes must scream the word - innovation.** Yes profit is essential. And a Bigger YES, innovation is absolutely essential to exploding profits.

27. **Launch a column called 'excellent failures' to include it in your employee appraisal.** Give it at least a 20% weightage.

28. **Diversity Is A Game Changer By Itself.** Black. White. Brown. Purple. Tall. Short. North. South. East. West. Asian. American. African. He. She. Public School. Private School. No School. College. Grad. Drop out.

29. **Women in exec-team. Women in every team by design.** This is not some 'social responsibility' project. Its a must for innovation. I can write a whole book on why women but I'll give you a reason here - Women purchase a half of all consumer and commercial products. And Women decide for half of the men too. So that's 75%.

30. **I am an enemy of mergers. They don't work. 99% of them don't.** But innovation **loves small acquisitions** that bring in a new wave of enterprise. A 2-person accounting firm with passion, a 10-person HR recruitment firm with expertise, a one-man sales training brilliance. You get the point.

31. **Celebration builds innovation culture.** Large, small, very small, even an irrelevant achievement is a big deal for someone else. Celebrate it.

32. **Celebrate failures.** Remember fast failure is the blood supply for innovation. It is critical. Don't make the mistake of making failure a mistake.

Customers

33. **Customers are the ears of innovation. Listen.** But lead too. Its not about slavish listening. But understanding before being understood.

34. **Customers on all teams. Especially the innovation crack

teams.

35. **The most valuable group - the angry pissed-off customers.** They are the ones with the highest expectations. That's what you are innovating for, anyway.

Collaboration

36. **Innovations fail, not because of the idea, but because of lack of cross-functional collaboration.** Be obsessed to create a culture that makes it a design to continuously interact with other functions.

37. **Cross Functional Innovators,** for example, a sales innovation project, in its team must have people representing all other functions.

38. **Cross Functional Friendships.** Institutionalize this. Friendships across functions are your best strategy yet. Foster it. Formally.

39. **Promotion to senior levels MUST be dependent on at least one cross-functional assignment - at least for a year.**

40. **Cross Functional Finance.** Managers must spend non-trivial time in Finance to understand the impact of their decisions on the business.

41. **Innovating organizations are a result of a collection of energetic and fearless project teams.** Innovations are never accomplished by teams designed from following the org-chart, that is by members who remain under the jurisdiction of their traditional bosses.

Projects

42. **Project Manager is your super star.** There are small number of superstars who must be retained at any cost. You already know who they are.

43. **HR Job #1.** Making projects successful.

44. **Projects about also managing the 'soft-stuff'** Remember *Projects* is not just about being clinical, mechanical and doing a job.

45. **If the project has failed, its not the team that is responsible, its the people to made that team who are.**

46. **Developing leaders (to create an innovating organization) is not about getting them ready for some designations (by doing some detailed competence BS analysis).** Teams are born. Teams die. Leaders will become followers and vice versa. Its not a joke, the analysis is a joke. Developing leaders is itself a skill. For example, You want leaders to lead innovation, which competency assessment tool or company will give you a score on that Hint: None. Experience of putting them through the grill, will give the result.

47. **If your org-chart makes absolute sense, then you don't have an innovative organization.** Question Your Assumptions. Build a culture of 'letting go'.

Centre For Excellence

48. **School within a school.** Setting up 'centers of excellence' that are run professionally and independently help immensely. For example, Samsung set up a complete Center of Excellence for

Global domination and gave Sony a run for their money in almost no time.

49. **Centre for excellence.** Market potential is enormous. Will dominate for next quarter century. Many "trying a few things." Advice: Don't mess around, get serious, and win big.

Decentralization

50. **This is number one innovation strategy. Big Company = Small Things.**

51. **Keep decentralizing.**

52. **Decentralize before it is needed.** This IS The KEY.

53. **Decentralization is an attitude, not a consulting project.**

The Top Team

54. **Innovation begins and ends with the Top Team.**

55. **Curiosity Quotient.** Curiosity may have killed the cat but the lack of it at top level kills the innovation.

56. **Innovation experience at the top - most don't have it and so they don't do it or support it.** Change things. Or add an Innovation officer.

57. **Diversity at the top.** Very rare. Fix it.

58. **Top Team Calendar Management.** If you are serious about innovation and if the people will take you seriously about innovation then it MUST show-up in your calendar every single

week.

59. **Chief Forgetting Officer.** Unlearning is key. Begin it with you.

60. **Beware of past glory.** Its a killer. When Steve Jobs re-arrived at Apple he tossed out all the models of yesterday's great "industry changing" computers—and replaced them with prototypes "from" tomorrow.

61. One last thing for Top Teams - **Innovation, essentially by definition, is about change before its needed.** Procrastination begins at the top. Procrastination reaches the bottom faster than raindrops hit the ground.

All or Nothing

62. **Innovation is fun or no fun.**

63. **Innovation is the way of life or not.**

64. **Innovation is scary (yes it is)**

65. **Innovation is enthusiasm.**

66. **Innovation is speed.**

67. **Innovation is Big**

68. **Innovation is small.**

69. Innovation **is** an iPod. Innovation **is also** a paper checklist that saves thousands of life at your neighboring hospital.

70. **Innovation is a movement.** Its a culture

Yes we all will not be Apple Inc. But we can damn well die trying. And that is a ride.

18

Is Your Organization Open To Change?
Section 4: Innovation & Change

Well, really there isn't much of a choice. Is it?

There are of course dozens of books and theories written on the subject and more will be. I want to take an over-simplified look at this. In my mind 300-page theories on change and adaptability are just that – theories. From my experience of very closely observing human behavior, I want to show the mirror to an organization's ability to change and its adaptability to it, in a few lines.

In my mind, if looked at solely from the point of view of adapting, slowing down of an organization's growth happens for two reasons.

1. **Failure to anticipate the changes that will occur and more importantly**

2. **Failure to adapt to the changes that occur or are occurring.**

Yes economies slow down and businesses do too. But not every business does. Some are agile enough to think, innovate and adapt. Others adapt too, though just not in time. They take a long time to accept or embrace the new, mostly because they take forever to let go off the old. Letting go of the old is more, much more critical to the process of change than embracing the new. The latter will almost always happen automatically.

Organizations take a long time to accept or embrace the new, mostly because they take forever to let go off the old.

There is ONE variable, just one to creating a fast and adaptable organization. This one variable is THE answer and has been THE answer for centuries. It is the only one that you have to deal with. It is no surprise.

Adaptability, Embracing change and MOST Importantly creating and leading change is 100% a function of people. How people are got on board, developed and appreciated, or not, will determine the organization's adaptability and its success.

Contrary to what you may think, neither the economy nor the industry dynamics of your market determines long-term success. How people anticipate and adapt to these factors determine success.

So here's my list. Anticipative and Adaptive (Successful) organizations **have people and team which,**

- **Are hired for attitude, character and teamwork (proven) much more than any skill or CV.**

- **Are visibly appreciated.**

- **Are treated with respect and dignity.** HINT: They are not crucified in review meetings, they are supported.

- **Are in the know of almost everything.** HINT: 'Need to know basis is old pseudo management.' Uncommon Sense – Transparency and Availability of Information is obviously a MUST if you have to anticipate and adapt to the coming change.

- **Are developed, and developed again, and again, and again to the power of infinity.** HINT: You can never spend enough time or money on training. If you think otherwise, read no further for figuring the reason for your slowdown.

- **Realize the power of NO (Don't > DO).** Stop doing certain things is much bigger than start doing new things.

- **Realize the power of YES.** Are willing to DO almost anything. That is giving it a shot! – HINT: BUT that will ONLY happen if failures are appreciated.

- **Learn new things everyday because that's the primary job. Period.**

- **Believe that everyone, every insider and every outsider has something to teach us.** HINT: Almost every person in your organization, including you is resistant to new learning without suspicion.

- **Are exposed to (as often as possible, perhaps everyday) to a wide variety of people who will offer radical and opposite views to the norm and convention.** HINT: If the norm and convention worked, there wouldn't be change needed ever.

- **Are given the freedom (with accountability) to try almost anything instantly and repeatedly. HINT:** Reward good and useful failures. Punish mediocre successes.

- **Are different, diverse, from every imaginable background.** A few, a handful in our country truly practices diversification by choice. Try it. It will shock you with its ROI.

- **Are self-accountable.** They treat everyone as indispensable. No threats. No non-players either. Everyone plays because failure is okay.

- Pursue breakthroughs and innovations (the real ones, not some bottom-line focused short-term gains) every day because that's the fun and that's the way my job was told to me.

- **Operate in a flat, non-bureaucratic, least hierarchical structure.**

- **Are honest.** BIG HINT: People lie (and then politics and corruption begins) because you have attached such a stigma to failure and mistakes. Grow Up.

And there it is.

- **Oh! One more….. all of this obviously requires 'leadership' that understands the people more than the business.** Business anyways slows down so didn't help to understand it, did it?

The Truth Remains – **if you and your people and the teams embraces the above practices – anticipation and adaptability will be so automatic that you wouldn't find yourself even using these words again.** Obviously I am exaggerating but you get the point.

An honest submission – This is so not a new idea. I wish I invented it but I didn't. However it's practice is so rare, that everyone else is researching the few who practice this. And that 'everyone else' is busy publishing 'theories on change or some BS like that'….. While all you need is Simplistic Common Sense.

And here it is one more time. Just n case I lost you.

Yes a BIG BURLY VISON is needed.
Yes a Detailed Strategy is great.
Yes Values are critical.
And Yes processes are a necessity.

BUT hey Einstein! In the end it **IS** and **ALWAYS** has been all about **THE PEOPLE.**

19

Damn HR

Section 4: Innovation & Change

Here are 17 questions to provoke and challenge the way you look at human beings. I am asking these questions through the lens of creating a 'transformation' – if you use a mediocre lens of 'let things go on' – then this isn't for you.

1. Are you at the heart of the **Brand Promise** 100% of the time?

   Talent = Brand.
   Brand can never be > What talent feels about it.

   Message: REAL Branding is personal. REAL Branding is integrity. REAL Branding is consistency & freshness. REAL Branding is the answer to WHO ARE WE? WHY ARE WE HERE? REAL Branding is why I/you/we [all] get out of bed in the morning. REAL Branding can't be faked. REAL Branding is a systemic, 24/7, all departments, all hands affair .

2. Have you considered that **HR can be the #1 source of market cap enhancement?** People are your #1 asset aren't they?

3. Do you recognize that your #1 job is to create a **Talent Development fanatics Team?**

4. Have your created a **truly diverse organization** or you following the herd from where you inherited the legacy?

5. Training and HR value proposition is the primary **Talent Attractant.** How are you using this?

6. Are your wary of weird people? Big mistake. **Pursue, train, encourage the weird is the way** to the breakthrough.
7. Do you embrace **or fight** the WCR – White-collar revolution?

8. Can you imagine **that your entire organization can be restructured** over night (almost) to do great work?

9. **90% of training and learning experiences will be internal to an organization in the next 5 years.** What are you doing about it?

10. **HR to HED?** Human Enablement Department.

11. **Training?** Violinists do it. Sprinters do it. Golfers do it. Pilots do it. Soldiers do it. Surgeons do it. Cops do it. Astronauts do it. Why don't businesspeople do it [very much]?

12. Drop training. Embrace learning. **Do you have a learning strategy?**

13. Drop learning. Embrace forgetting. **What are you doing for unlearning in the organization?**

    Forget > "Learn"   - "The problem is never how to get new, innovative thoughts into your mind, but how to get the old ones out." -   Dee Hock

14. **How do you train for ambiguity?**

    "There will be more confusion in the business world in the next decade than in any decade in history. And the current pace of change will only accelerate."   - Steve Case

15. Are you focused on **Boss-Free implementation of STM (stuff that matters)** or are you stuck in hierarchical, medieval way of doing business?

16. Is your HR department **unique?** Or is it a **replica of industry standard.**
    "The 'surplus society' has a surplus of **similar** companies,

employing **similar** people, with **similar** educational backgrounds, coming up with **similar** ideas, producing **similar** things, with **similar** prices and **similar** quality." - Kjell Nordstrom and Jonas Ridderstrale, Funky Business

17. What's your **WOW** project?

18. Are you or creating and promoting certified **RADICALS?**

    "If things seem under control, you're just **not** going fast enough." - Mario Andretti

    "I'd rather regret the things I have done than the things I have **not**." - Lucille Ball

    "If you ask me what I have come to do in this world, I who am an artist, I will reply, I am here to **live my life out loud**." - Emile Zola

    Have you **changed civilization today**? - Source: HP banner ad

    "Let's **make a dent** in the universe." - Steve Jobs

20
I Am Responsible
Section 4: Innovation & Change

The easiest thing to do in this world is to blame. Another easy thing to do is self-pity. I truly don't know which of these is easier. I do know that either of them leads to a wasted, idiotic and a joyless life.

Think about it - Wouldn't it be cool if all politicians weren't allowed to blame anybody else, and had to take full responsibility for their own actions and results?

That's how change would happen. That's how change happens when it does.

- You have a rough day at work - **you blame the boss!**
- You have a rough day at home - **you blame the spouse!**
- You have long hours - **you blame the company!**
- Your company isn't doing well - **you blame the economy!**
- You are gaining weight - **you blame work-life balance!**
- You run short of money - **you blame the inflation!**
- You aren't happy - **you blame everything around you!**

You blame, blame, blame - and then you wallow in self-pity because you feel that you've got a raw deal.

Wait!

Everyone who ever lived on this planet got a raw deal. Life wasn't easy for anyone because its life. People had exactly the same circumstances like you or even worse. Yet some rose to greatness. BIG SECRET - they didn't find the comfort of blame and self-pity.

I am not over simplifying. That's the fact. Here's an exact look at the 'what is'. This is the reality –

- You have a rough day at work - **you CHOSE your job.**

- You have a rough day at home - **you CHOSE your spouse (or chose silence when your spouse was chosen).**
- You have long working hours - **you CHOOSE to be at work than at home.**
- Your company isn't doing well - **your company CHOSE it's decisions.**
- You are gaining weight - **you CHOOSE what goes in your mouth, every single time.**
- You run short of money - **you CHOOSE to swipe that credit card.**
- You aren't happy - **you CHOSE everything above. This is the outcome.**

I am quite sick of people telling me that there life is what it is because of - job, pressure, family, economy, time, upbringing, society, country - These are bloody lame excuses.

As you read those excuses, they seem kind of lame don't they? Are they lame? Or are they pathetic excuses?

The line between childhood and adulthood is crossed when we move from saying, "it got lost" to "I lost it"

The transition from leading a mediocre life to living an abundant life happens through taking responsibility and realizing that you are the one driving your life. If its in a particular state, its in that state ONLY because of you.

Think about it - if you find blame, then the change will happen only when the other side changes. That's sad. You can wait your whole life for that but no one is going to change to make your life better. Won't happen.

Responsibility is our ability to respond to circumstances and to choose the attitudes, actions, and reactions that shape our lives. It is a concept of power that puts us in the driver's seat. The grand panorama of the potential of our lives can only be appreciated when we begin to be accountable and self-reliant.

Whether you're in politics or not, the burden is the same: take responsibility for all that happens. And if it's not happening in the best way possible, take responsibility to make it happen in a better way.

It's funny how you can picture responsibility and blame in terms of a politician. Can you imagine a politician saying, "The bill didn't pass and it was all my fault." Could you ever imagine that in your lifetime?

Aren't you sick of blaming? Aren't you sick of politicians blaming each other ad nauseam for what the other guy didn't do? Isn't there a biblical phrase that begins, **"Let he who was without sin cast the first stone"**?

Let me tell you a story -

There once was this important football game between two teams. One teams was much larger than the other. The larger team was dominating the game and beating the smaller team. The coach for the smaller team saw that his team was not able to contain or block the larger team. So his only hope was to call the plays that went to Calhoun, the fastest back in the team who could easily outrun the larger players once he broke free.

The coach talked with his quarterback about giving the ball to Calhoun and letting him run with it. The first play the coach was excited, but Calhoun did not get the ball. The second play was again signaled for Calhoun, but once again Colhoun did not get the ball. Now the game was in the final seconds with the smaller teams only hope being for Calhoun to break free and score the winning touchdown. The third play and again Calhoun did not get the ball. The coach was very upset so he sent in the play again for the fourth and final play. The ball was snapped and the quarterback was sacked, ending the game. The coach was furious as he confronted the quarterback: "I told you four times to give the ball to Calhoun and now we've lost the game."

The quarterback stood tall and told the coach, "Four times I called the play to give the ball to Calhoun. **The problem was that Calhoun did not want the ball.**"

That's your truth.

You don't want the ball.

Because when you take the ball, you got to run and do the hard work. You got to make the pace and you got to lead and change the game.

And you aren't ready for that and so you create a life full of excuses. You don't want to change the game. You want to exist, as is. And then you wonder why it doesn't work for you.

Sad.

Life is simple. Success is simple. Breakthroughs are simple. There is just one thing to do.

TAKE THE BALL AND RUN!

Take responsibility and change.

Yes, you could be thinking 'but it's not my fault' - okay agreed. But so what? Whose life is getting affected? and who will change it?

HERE'S THE REALITY: If you want to live and not merely exist, you have to realize that, "I am responsible because I want to live. No excuses. No blame. No self-pity. It's my ball, I will take it and run."

Yes, there are barriers. There are circumstances. And all of those barriers and circumstances would disappear if you take responsibility, choose your life another way and run with it.

Or you can just blame and whine and simply exist to be forgotten. Like a politician.

21
Life Is Not A Spectator Sport
Section 4: Innovation & Change

If you aren't growing, you are dying.

This isn't philosophy. Its logic. Really. The only time we cease to grow is upon death. Till then in some measure we grow.

Reading the logic conversely it simply says that if we have ceased to proactively grow, we have begun to proactively die or at least kill a part of us.

So therein lies an answer to life. Progress is the only way to lasting happiness. If you are moving forward, you are happy. Stagnation, waiting for things to change, leads you to an opposite end. A sad one full of blame, pity and reasons.

Let me give you a few thoughts on how we are spectators. Its sad...

- watchers instead of doers
- 'wait and watch. lets take one step at a time'
- consumers instead of creators
- 'I could have done it better'... Could have in which life?
- observers instead of participants
- 'I knew it wouldn't work'
- watch others sing instead of singing
- listen to stories instead of sharing your own

"Life is not a spectator sport. If you're going to spend your whole life in the grandstand just watching what goes on, in my opinion you're wasting your life."- -Jackie Robinson

Think about this too - If you are a spectator, what you do best is observe and criticize.

- You are not playing.

- So you don't need any help.
- So you don't get any.
- Life wouldn't change for you.
- And sadly but quickly you'll be irrelevant.

Like it or not. Life is in progress. Its not waiting. You may be a spectator. That doesn't mean that the game isn't on. It simply means that **you are so scared to lose, you rather just watch.**

Everything else except for the present moment is uncertain. Wouldn't it be wiser to live it? Play it?

Don't wait. Don't blame. Don't pity. - We have limited moments in this lifetime. They are passing us by.

If not now, when will you live, play?

22

The Great Salespeople

Section 5: Sales & Marketing

Sachin Tendulkar in one of his press conferences made a brilliant statement. He said that when you're on top of your game then retiring at that moment is selfish because that is the time that you better be serving your nation.

I thought that was a gem. Its high standard stuff.

What standards have you set?

I am writing this here for salespeople, for greatness in salespeople. **If you are not in sales, you must read this because you are always in sales.**

1. **Know the product.** Find the old warhorses in the company and absorb everything.

2. **Know the company,** specifically the culture.

3. **Know the customer.** Everything about them. Most important to know - their culture.

4. **Go viral.** Spread your relationships across functions and designations within your organization.

5. **Go viral #2.** Spread your relationships across your customers' organizations.

6. **Love politics** within your company. Its a reality. Love. Embrace it. Master it.

7. **Respect competition.** They have a share of the market not without reason, now learn why.

8. **Integrity Selling.** Sell only (ONLY) if it is solving a problem.

9. **Make it your problem to solve the problem.** No matter whom you need to find to solve the problem, find. That's the best way to cement a long-term relationship.

10. **Do not compromise.** Compromise is not a solution. It is a compromise.

11. **Work within a set of values.** Have your own. Stick to them. So you know when to say No.

12. **Create your own brand that is your name.** How? Be an expert. Start writing. It doesn't need skill. It needs discipline.

13. **Act as an 'orchestra - conductor'.** Reason is simple. You are responsible even if the other guy screws up. Always you.

14. **Constantly add value to the customer beyond your organization's product or service.**

15. Walk away from bad business even if it loses you your job. Learning to say 'NO' in a sales career is learning to 'Lead'.

16. **Understand the idea of a 'good loss'.** Its better to let someone else live with a bad business. Have your focus clear. This will emanate once you have your own values.

17. **Develop a mindset that those who say 'price issue, price, price, price!!!' just haven't understood you yet.** So you will start again every-time they say 'price'.

18. **No will always be a starting position.** Stop dropping your head every time you here it. Your career begins because there is that position.

19. The difference between great salespeople and mediocre salespeople is not their closure rates, **the difference is that the great ones always have a pipeline of leads.**

20. **Seek customers who are demanding what your product doesn't have.** Now you will stretch. And make everyone do so.

21. **Be an equal** to a customer, a vendor, your leader, anyone. You are no lesser human being. Practice 'partnership' obsessively. Be a partner. Equal partner.

22. **Thank You.** The most powerful emotion yet. Send thank you notes (not the silly e-notes). When you do send them, write 'WE'.

23. When you look across the table have this attitude - for example in my line of work it is, "**How can I get this company a breakthrough** and get him or her promoted?"

24. **Have you made a difference to those you met today?** Make sure you can answer yes every single evening.

25. Keep your bloody **PowerPoint slides** (if you must keep them at all) **simple and minimal.**

26. **Opportunism (with a heart) mostly wins.** The greatest ones are good at Plan-B.

27. **Nothing succeeds the first time.** Absolutely Nothing. What are you made off?

28. **If No 'Wow' then No 'Go'.**
29. **Speed.** Speed on solutions. Speed on sending that proposal.

Speed on delivery. Speed on excellence. Speed differentiates. Bosses and Clients love speed.

30. A startling discovery - Harvard's study on the 100 Most Top Performing Salespeople of the World revealed that they **ALL woke up at 5AM to exercise and read.**

31. Micromanage to the last degree - your first and last impressions.

32. The biggest key to outsell competition and your own colleagues - **Ask Better and More Intelligent Questions.**

33. Can't stress this enough. **Good listeners are good salespeople.** Period.

34. **Great listeners are Great Salespeople. Period.**

35. A big secret to winning. **Outread Everyone else.** Outread the competition, the clients, the colleagues, and the leaders. Outread to Outdo. Works 100% of the time.

36. **Are you a great interviewer?** It's a make or break skill.

37. **Are you a great (not good) presenter?** It can have a stupendous payoff to your life. It's really funny this. I know no one, who unless dragged by his company would go and master the skill. And yet in your corporate life this is one skill that subjects you to most judgment.

38. **Under promise even if it costs you business.** Do it as a rule. Winning is a long-term affair.

39. **Keep your word.** Always. Especially on 'time' commitments.

40. **People keep looking for product or service differentiators.** Here is one - Do more homework than the next guy and you'll position yourself as an expert automatically.

41. **Everyone should win, or, it wasn't a good sale.** Hint - I must feel I have won.

42. REPEAT - **He or She with most number of good relationships will have most number of wins.**

43. **Phones beat email.**

44. **Lend a helping hand to your client especially when you don't have the time.** You now have a client for life.

45. **Enthusiasm** is as important as any skill.

46. Your single-minded goal in building a sales career - **Work like hell to build a reputation of an expert.**

47. **Be kind.** Even if you are from the corner office at GE.

48. **Think 'Turnkey'** - Everything is your problem.

49. **Work on your story.** A better story outsells a better product.

50. **Luck Matters.** So Get Lucky by doing all this. Good Luck.

51. **Give value first.** Give value before. Give value after. But most importantly Give Value Before anything.

52. **Don't use closing techniques you were taught in your sales training.** Customer smells manipulation.

53. **Don't ask questions which are none of your business.** For example about money.

54. **Don't compare yourself to the competition.** You establish leadership with the other company by doing that.

55. **Don't try to find pain points.** Focus on building rapport. Rest will follow as an outcome.

56. **Don't meet a non-decision-maker.** Why would you?

57. **Don't ever discuss prejudices.** Example- religion, gender, geographies. Not acceptable.

58. **Don't make excuses for what went wrong.** People don't like to buy from those who make excuses. Check out and reflect on your buying experiences.

59. **Don't forget to Google yourself.** Your customer will do it.

60. **Don't ever make the mistake of analyzing that a customer didn't buy because price was the issue.** The failure is yours on convincing him or her of the value.

61. **Cold calls are annoying.** If you are still making them, well you are welcome to stay put in 1980s. Move over. Referrals, Networking, Social Networking, all yes, Cold Calls are annoying. Period.

62. **Sales is Engagement.** Telling is not selling. Create a question based strategy versus 'a tell all 'strategy.

63. REPEAT: **Attitude and Enthusiasm** will out-perform any strategy.

64. **Most salespeople don't have a value proposition.** They have a sales pitch. Be HIGHLY aware that value is what the client perceives. Pitch is what you offer and that is immaterial to the other side.

65. **Don't be in meetings to make sales.** Its not worth it. Make relationships. The reason is simple –

66. **Sales are made emotionally and then justified logically. Always.** You, yourself never bought a car, clothing, pen, computer, grocery, anything because the ROI appealed to you. Did you?

So once again just to make sure you have understood what I have been saying here,

67. **Objections occur in sales presentations.** So if you want to eliminate all sales objections, eliminate the sales pitch. Concentrate on gaining and building rapport.

68. **Yes, some customers will always just buy lowest price.** I recommend you give those customers to your competitor, in order that they may make no profit.

69. **Don't hang around negative people.** Please surround yourself and your time with people who are positive. The bickering blamers - Give it a miss unless you want your career to be set back by about 20 years.

70. **PICTURE THIS:** Your boss says, "Make 100 cold calls this week." And the first 20 people you call hang up on you.
    PICTURE THIS: You have one prospect left this month and if they don't buy, you don't make your target. They call you

and say, "We've decided to buy from your competition."

PICTURE THIS: You finally get an appointment with the biggest prospect you've ever had. They've agreed to see you for one hour. You arrive and the decision maker doesn't show up.

Those are all real -world sales occurrences that every one of you has experienced. **RESILIENCE** is how you react, respond, and recover from those situations and,

71. One quality that will take you over the line - **have a bloody sense of humor**. I run into these situations and I find them funny. Sometimes you get a raw deal for no fault of yours - would a smile make you feel better than a curse?

72. **Always do the right thing over and above the acceptable thing** - you'll have lifetime of success. Sometimes the right thing for the client is to not buy from you.

73. **Eliminate 'other peoples drama' from your life and you have an additional 24hrs to sell.**

Here are a few painful questions to ponder over.

Do you spend more time on other people's drama in office or your career?

Other people's drama in the neighborhood or your children?

Other people's drama (criticizing their attempts to market themselves) or building your personal brand?

Other people's drama (gossiping the 'what if' and 'why' they get or not got promoted) or your success?

Other people's drama (on the television) or your own intimate relationships? (ouch!)

74. **Don't ever say to yourself, 'I don't have the time'** - The most self-defeating statement to make. In fact you have accepted defeat even before trying.

75. For this last one, here are a few approaches and strategies that I try to use. I am listing them down. See how many of them are yours. Use it as you may. **A final checklist perhaps..**

    o I have done my homework about their company.
    o I have done my homework on the person I'm meeting with.
    o I'm prepared with questions of engagement about them.
    o I'm prepared with ideas in their favor.
    o I'm more relaxed than formal.
    o I'm confident, not cocky.
    o I'm more friendly than professional.
    o I give signed books, not brochures.
    o I don't start until I have established rapport AND found common ground.
    o I listen more and talk less.
    o I walk into the sales call with ideas, and questions, not a pitch.
    o I look for their pleasure, not for their pain.
    o I don't talk about what "we do." I talk about how they win.
    o I ask for and get their 'bucket' list (what they're hoping to achieve).
    o I discover my customer's reasons and motives for buying.
    o I answer with questions, not just statements.
    o I dare to inject humor. Often. Not jokes, humor.
    o I don't make presentations from my laptop – I don't use slides - I use myself - If I must, if I use slides it's from a projector.
    o If I use slides, they're fun and they're customized for the prospect.
    o I make my own slides.
    o I often clarify a statement with a question before I answer.

- I discuss money openly (it's my favorite part).
- I listen with the intent to understand, and then respond.
- I use testimonials to prove points and create a buying atmosphere.
- I am more patient than anxious. I wait for them to ask, then tell.
- When I hear a buying signal, I ask for, and confirm the sale.
- I don't leave without asking for the sale or formalizing the next step.

23

50 Key Lessons In Sales And In Marketing

Section 5: Sales &Marketing

I have been consulting and coaching business leaders for almost two decades. **Here are 50 Lessons, Questions, and Provocations that I have found to work the most. Try them. It's great stuff.**

1. **Are your goals worthy of you?** if you are asking the opposite question, you have already lost the plot.

2. **What don't I know that is absolutely critical to my success?**

3. **How can I personally make my clients' life better?**

4. **Find or pick a charity you personally believe in.**

5. **Start building a dream team.**

6. **Create a Stadium Pitch.** If you had a packed stadium full of people who could take you to the next level, and had only 30 seconds with them, what will you say? They can leave anytime !! - and that's the reality, you are ALWAYS in a Stadium Pitch situation in life.

7. **Fundamentally there are only three ways to grow a business** - Increase Clients, Increase the average sales price, and Increase the number of times they buy from you. What assumptions is your business making? Are they right?

8. **Use an all-base approach to marketing:** much like a war - air, land, and water - all at once. Create Impact.

9. **Test your ideas. Don't assume either way.**

10. **Be your prospect.** Get an experience of buying from you. Invaluable.

11. **What is your magnificent obsession?** What is so deeply attractive about you and your business that it attracts people?

12. **Your customers are marketing geniuses** - they know what they want and its your job to find out.

13. **Always follow your gut feelings, intuition and instincts - more than analytics.**

14. **What would you do differently if your business were treated like a movie theatre?** Admission fee is charged at entry and the word travels like lightening whether its a hit or flop? How's your movie?

15. **Are your customer relations such that they refer you?** HINT: they refer either way. In a good way or bad? Referrals or Word of mouth are key to exponential success. No business has grown exponentially without this.

16. **Think about lifetime value of your clients.** Not quarterly.

17. **Ask who else does business with my client?** What are my opportunities here?

18. **If you are in retail business -** the only differentiator is experience!!

19. **Set the buying criteria for your customers** - can you fulfill them from thereon.

20. **Plan your long-term strategies before you plan this years' tactics.**

21. **Use risk reversal.** If you cant offer to your clients / customers

that dissatisfaction = no money to be paid - no questions asked, then you are plain inefficient.

22. **Is my business a refreshing alternate to others?** if not, then why do it?

23. **When you fall in love with your clients (their enjoyment from your business) more than your business, you have it figured.**

24. **Are you living your business values?** If not, you are pursuing wrong ones!

25. **Do you have a one-page business strategy that proves that your exponential success?** If not (in one page and that simple) it won't happen.

26. **Call back all those people who said NO to you for what you wanted from them?** You'll convert at least 25%.

27. **Learn to barter.** Its a great tool for growth.

28. **Dare.** Dare to break industry norms completely.

29. **Follow hunches.** Proof isn't needed.

30. **Start with outrageous claims and challenges.** Worry about meeting them and fulfilling them from thereon.

31. **Always ALWAYS remember that if you don't do it someone half as smart and half as nice will do it.**

32. **Create an itch they have to scratch -** otherwise its not a USP yet!

33. **Always communicate what you are about to do and why -** its essential in a sales situation.

34. **Small improvements leveraged by technology leads to breakthroughs.** Technologies simply introduced because its an 'in-thing' leads to breakdowns.

35. **Forget about inside the box or outside the box thinking.** Its still a box. Get rid of the box. Look elsewhere.

36. **Write a book.** Because everyone can.

37. **Write down every objection your salespeople ever heard.** Script it.

38. **Write down a sales script where you bring up the objection before your clients do.**

39. **Always remember to up-sell.** Don't be satisfied.

40. **Create momentum in your business.** Yes, have stability with some core offering but have something new each month. Keep alive!

41. **Would you sell your offering to your mother, father, son, and daughter?** Really? If not, then get out of this job or business or fix it.

42. **Do you send out catalogs or marketing gifts to clients or associates?** Do you send some call to sales action in it? If not you have lost 30-300% increase.

43. **Barter your knowledge.** Treat it as barter of power.
44. **If you must, try to hire consultants who have NO**

Knowledge of your industry. Knowledge of the core subject, that's it.

45. **Test your old-methods that used to work but stopped working.** There are hidden breakthroughs. Everything is cyclical.

46. **Do not interact with anyone unless you can improve his or her life.** Its a waste for you and them.

47. **Work in time chunks.** Multi-tasking kills excellence.

48. **What's the one thing you learnt yesterday?** Ask yourself this question everyday. If you find yourself saying nothing or just shrugging your shoulders everyday - YOU need serious change!

49. **Ask what you don't want in life and business.** Then get to what you want.

50. **Take Action TODAY.**

24
Presentation Excellence
Section 5: Sales &Marketing

"The problem with communication …is the ILLUSION that it has been accomplished" —George Bernard Shaw

1. **Total commitment to the Problem/Project/Outcome**

2. **A compelling "Story line"/"Plot"**

3. **Enough data to sink a tanker** (98% in reserve)

4. **Know the data from memory (not from slides);** ability to manipulate the data in your head

5. **Great Stories/Illustrations/Vignettes**

6. **Superb "political antennae"** - you must be hyper-attentive to the likes of Body Language)

7. By hook or by crook - **Connect**

8. **Connect. Connect. Connect**

9. **Get inside the head of your audience for the duration of your speech.**

10. **Punch line/ Plot Outline/ WOW/ Surprise in first one to two minutes or you'll lose.** Once you've "won" … stop pushing (don't "rub it in").

11. **Be "in command" but don't "show off"** (if you're brilliant they'll figure it out for themselves). If you need to show it, you probably aren't brilliant. Don't try either way.

12. **Pay attention to the Senior Person present,** but not too much

(don't look like/act like/be a "suck-up").

13. **Brief the hell out of your "champions" before the presentation;** insist that they make changes/fine tune. They must "own" the outcome before the fact!

14. **Don't try to "score off" your detractors.** Be especially courteous to them (even if/especially if they're jerks)

15. Adjust as you go: **Let the groups arrive at your conclusion, they must own it.** ("I knew that") **In the end!** ~ this is a special skill and takes practice.

16. **No more than 3 key points!** Come at them in several different ways.

17. **No more than ONE point per slide!**

18. **Slides: No Clutter** (no wee print/ charts/graphs)

19. **Slides: Good quotes from the field.** (Remember you're "telling a story")

20. **Be aware of differing cognitive styles, especially M-F.**

21. **There must be "surprise."** Some key facts that are not commonly known are counter-intuitive (no reason to do the presentation in the first place if there are no Surprises).

22. **Summarize the argument/story from time to time .**

23. **Include an Action Agenda that involves some small items that will be started/accomplished in the next 72 hours** (this

ices commitment/practicality) [SEP]

24. **If you don't know something - Admit it! -** This is actually a good thing—as opposed to appearing as a "know it all"

25. **Ask for the sale.** (Remember to be a "closer")

26. **This *is* War** (a war for Hearts & Mind), but never forget that you are the Supplicant!

27. **Data are imperative, but also play to Emotion.**

28. **Consider bringing along a "customer" (internal or perhaps external) for support.**

29. **Be precisely clear where/when you intend to prototype** - and that the prototype guinea pig is lined up (better yet, do the first, at least partial, prototype before the presentation)

30. **Compromise but don't yield!**

31. Assume that you may be cut off at any moment, and be prepared to give on the spot a compelling 30-second to one- minute (no longer!) **Brilliant Summary including Sales Pitch**

32. **Follow the Law of Recency:** Make sure that you have been in the field with the key "operating" players more recently than anyone in the room.

33. **Make it clear that you've done a Staggering Amount of Homework,** even though you are exhibiting but a tiny fraction - allude to the tons of research that are available if desired by participants; offer deeper one-on-one briefings if desired.

34. **Smile! Relax** (to a point) (fake it if necessary) ("up tight" is disastrous) (remember you are doing them a favor by sharing this **Compelling Opportunity!**)

35. **Eye Contact!**

36. **Be shrewd:** Override some interruptions; be attentive to others (distraction is okay and normal ... within limits!).

37. **Becoming an Excellent Presenter is as tough as becoming a great baseball pitcher.** This is important and Presentation Excellence is never accidental!

38. **Practice** - but don't leave your game in the locker room.

39. **Seek tips on how various participants** "play the [presentation] game"

40. **A Presentation is an Act** (FDR: "The President must be the nation's number one actor")

41. **Remember, the presentation is about Change-** Resistance is normal - in fact if there's no resistance then your Project is hardly a "game changer"

42. **Dress well. Don't over-dress.** The only rule that applies here – Both sides should be comfortable with what you're wearing.

43. **Be early.** Obvious but worth saying.

44. **Get the A/V right, perfect.** Its your job.

45. **Don't bring a partner without a role.** Its shabby and indicates desperation and idleness.

46. **No matter how good you are you'll have crappy days. Get back to work. Weep if you need to but get back quick.**

47. **Speak in "Plain English"** – even if you're presenting to the Queen.

48. **Make your Personal Commitment clear as a bell!**

49. **Emphasize "competitive advantage" and timeliness (act now),** without stooping to ridiculous war-like language ("tear the heart out of the competition"). In audiences with heavy female component, if you are male, avoid repetitive "football analogues")

50. **Underscore the USP/Unique Selling Proposition.**

51. **Emphasize the Positive.**

52. **Sell Novelty yet "fit" with "core values"** - One of the biggest mistakes in a presentation to be found to be against a 'value system' of the audience.

53. **Remember JFK's** immortal words: **"The only reason to give a speech is to change the world"**

54. **Say what you have to say Clearly ... and then Say It Again & Again from slightly different angles.**

55. **Make it clear that you are a Man/Woman of Action** - and Execution Excellence is your First, Middle, and Last Name!

56. Energy! Enthusiasm!

57. Enjoy it! This is a Hoot! THE ULTIMATE TURN ON!
Remember your Goal: Change the world!

"In classical times when Cicero had finished speaking, the people said, 'How well he spoke,' but when Demosthenes had finished speaking, they said, 'Let us march.'"   —Adlai Stevenson

Let us march.

25
Top Quotes

1. "Do one thing every day that scares you." —Eleanor Roosevelt

2. "Life is either a daring adventure, or nothing."—Helen Keller

3. "Tell me, what is it you plan to do with your one wild and precious life?" —Mary Oliver

4. "Dream as if you'll live forever. Live as if you'll die today."—James Dean

5. "The two most powerful things in existence: a kind word and a thoughtful gesture."—Ken Langone, founder, Home Depot

6. "The deepest human need is the need to be appreciated."—William James

7. "Don't belittle!" —OD Consultant, on the essence of a well-functioning human community "If you don't listen, you don't sell anything." —Carolyn Marland/MD/Guardian Group

8. "It was much later that I realized Dad's secret. He gained respect by giving it. He talked and listened to the fourth-grade kids in Spring Valley who shined shoes the same way he talked and listened to a bishop or a college president. He was seriously interested in who you were and what you had to say." —Sara Lawrence-Lightfoot, *Respect*

9. "What creates trust, in the end, is the leader's manifest respect for the followers." — Jim O'Toole, *Leading Change*

10. "If you can't state your position in eight words or less, you don't have a position." —Seth Godin

11. "Never doubt that a small group of committed people can change the world. Indeed it is the only thing that ever has." —Margaret Mead

12. "Make your life itself a creative work of art." —Mike Ray, *The Highest Goal*

13. "Have you invested as much this year in your career as in your car?" —Molly Sargent, OD consultant and trainer

14. "If you don't like change, you're going to like irrelevance even less." —General Eric Shinseki, retired Chief of Staff, U. S. Army

15. "You must be the change you wish to see in the world." —Gandhi

16. "We eat change for breakfast!" —Harry Quadracci, founder, QuadGraphics

17. "If things seem under control, you're just not going fast enough." —Mario Andretti

18. "You can't behave in a calm, rational manner. You've got to be out there on the lunatic fringe." —Jack Welch, retired CEO, GE

19. "We have a 'strategic' plan. It's called doing things." —Herb Kelleher, founder, Southwest Airlines

20. "I guess it comes down to a simple choice, really. Get busy

living, or get busy dying." —The Shawshank Redemption (Tim Robbins)

21. "The most successful people are those who are good at plan B." —James Yorke, mathematician, on chaos theory in The New Scientist

22. "Tom, what have you done this year?" —Jessica Sutherland, Director, Institute for International Research/Middle East (TP: "Yikes!")

23. "To live is the rarest thing in the world. Most people exist, that is all." —Oscar Wilde

24. "People want to be part of something larger than themselves. They want to be part of something they're really proud of, that they'll fight for, sacrifice for, that they trust." —Howard Schultz, Starbucks

25. "It is not the strongest of the species that survives, nor the most intelligent, but the one most responsive to change." —Charles Darwin

26. "We may not be interested in chaos but chaos is interested in us." —Robert Cooper, The Breaking of Nations: Order and Chaos in the Twenty-first Century

27. "A man without a smiling face must not open a shop." —Chinese Proverb

28. "Stay Hungry. Stay Foolish." —Steve Jobs, Apple

29. "Groups become great only when everyone in them, leaders and members alike, is free to do his or her absolute best."

—Warren Bennis and Patricia Ward Biederman, Organizing Genius

30. "The best thing a leader can do for a Great Group is to allow its members to discover their greatness."—Warren Bennis and Patricia Ward Biederman, Organizing Genius

31. "You are the storyteller of your own life, and you can create your own legend or not." —Isabel Allende

32. "Nobody can prevent you from choosing to be exceptional." —Mark Sanborn, *The Fred Factor*

33. "A leader is a dealer in hope." —Napoleon

34. "Nothing is so contagious as enthusiasm." —Samuel Taylor Coleridge

35. "The greatest danger for most of us is not that our aim is too high and we miss it, but that it is too low and we reach it." – Michelangelo

36. "If you're enthusiastic about the things you're working on, people will come ask you to do interesting things." —James Woolsey, former CIA director

37. "Before you can inspire with emotion, you must be swamped with it yourself. Before you can move their tears, your own must flow. To convince them, you must yourself believe." —Winston Churchill

38. "If your actions inspire others to dream more, learn more, do more and become more, you are a leader." —John Quincy Adams

39. "A year from now you may wish you had started today." — Karen Lamb

40. Repeat from an earlier chapter (because its worth repeating) A man approached JP Morgan, held up an envelope, and said, "Sir, in my hand I hold a guaranteed formula for success, which I will gladly sell you for $25,000."

"Sir," JP Morgan replied, "I do not know what is in the envelope, however if you show me, and I like it, I give you my word as a gentleman that I will pay you what you ask."

The man agreed to the terms, and handed over the envelope. JP Morgan opened it, and extracted a single sheet of paper. He gave it one look, a mere glance, then handed the piece of paper back to the gent.

And paid him the agreed-upon $25,000.

1. Every morning, write a list of the things that need to be done that day.

2. **Do Them.**